MAXIMISE
YOUR
POTENTIAL

R. Ian Seymour

wrightbooks

Dedicated to "Doodoo" with much love...

CONTENTS

PREFACE

ROBERT IAN COLLIER died some 30 years ago. He was a well-liked and highly respected individual who lived a long, happy and very successful life. Robert was a wealthy businessman, but his real passion in life was in the field of self-help and personal development. Robert was also a dedicated family man who just also happened to take a shine to me. You see, Robert was my uncle. In fact, I am named after him, although I'm known mostly by my middle name, Ian, rather than Robert.

I lost my own father when I was very young and Uncle Bob, as I used to call him, became my mentor. He was always there to encourage and inspire me and he taught me everything I know about sales, about business and about how to succeed in the game of life. He was my teacher, my personal mentor and my very own Jiminey Cricket. I think that everyone should have an Uncle Bob in their life, no matter how old they are, and that's the reason I wrote this book — so that I might pass on what was given to me.

I like to talk *to* people rather than talk *at* people, and I have tried to write this book in the same way, so that it will talk to you. My intention, through these pages, is to reach out in a personal way and offer guidance, advice and, most of all, encouragement, which is exactly what Uncle Bob did for me. To help achieve this aim, each chapter of the book is written in the form of a letter from me to you.

Now the chances are that I don't know you personally, but the very fact that you have picked this book up and are reading these words tells me that you are a go-getter, a person seeking self-improvement and success. For the duration of your reading, then, I shall refer to you as "Dear Go-getter" (a term my uncle often used when referring to me) and I shall be your personal mentor, your Jiminey Cricket or, if you will, your very own Uncle Bob.

Robert Ian Seymour
February 1999

CHAPTER ONE

Persistence Conquers Resistance

Dear Go-getter,

MY INTENTION IN these letters is to share with you some of my insights for winning and achieving lasting results in this game of life. In this first letter, I want to talk about endurance and the power of persistence. However, before we start, I would like to make you aware of, and warn you against, the biggest obstacle standing in the way of success: discouragement.

Discouragement is by far the biggest killer of accomplishment known to man. In fact, the word "dis" (being the prefix indicating reversal, negation and removal) is derived from the Roman god of the same name, Dis (also called Orcas or Pluto), who was the god of the underworld, Hades: the abode of the dead. The story goes that Dis, the so-called god of discouragement, is also dishonest. He is a liar and a cheat and he deceives many to believe that he doesn't really exist, so that they will not be on their guard against him. However, far from being dead, he and his accomplices are alive and well, and roam the earth devouring mankind and feeding on its hope. The greatest defence against Dis, therefore, is to acknowledge

1

to yourself that he does, in fact, exist, and then resist his attempts to discourage you. You see, the one thing that discouragement cannot stand against is endurance, or persistence.

Persistence is the main attribute common to all successful people. To persist in the face of adversity is the single most important factor in determining the success or failure of any venture. At the end of the day, it doesn't really matter what it is that you try to do; if you just work at it long enough and hard enough, you will eventually succeed. Let me put it this way: persistence always conquers resistance ... eventually.

As an example, let me share with you a personal experience which demonstrates this little slogan perfectly. In November 1992, after almost 12 months of writing, writing off and rewriting, the finished manuscript of my first book, *One on One Selling*, finally lay on my desk. I soon found out that writing the book had been the easy part. Getting it published proved to be a completely different story. It took another 18 months — until March 1994 — along with what can only be described as a constant barrage of rejections, before the manuscript finally became a book.

Today, I am completely convinced that my success as an author came about, not because of some extraordinary talent, but simply because of my sheer persistence and my refusal to accept defeat. Of course, that is not to say there weren't times when I felt utterly dejected. Indeed, on several occasions, the thought occurred to me that I was flogging a dead horse and just wasting my time. Often, I considered giving up, but I would only allow myself to entertain such thoughts briefly, before I would shake the thought from my head and push on again, always believing deep down that mine was a worthwhile venture.

Over that 18-month period, I came to understand what real rejection is. I kept a record of the publishers I had contacted: all in all, I received over 70 rejections before I eventually succeeded. I now know and understand why so many talented would-be authors fall by the wayside.

However, I have also come to understand that, whether it is 18 months or 18 years, persistence always conquers resistance, eventually. At the time of writing this letter, *One on One Selling* has now been translated into five different languages. The book is also published in 12 different countries and, judging from the regular letters I receive, it has been, and continues to be, a benefit to many thousands of people all over the world. This, I believe, has nothing to do with luck or good fortune or any extraordinary talent on my part, but simply to a dogged determination and persistence.

As I've already said, it doesn't matter what it is that you try to do, if you just work at it hard enough and long enough you will eventually succeed — provided, of course, that you have some talent for it ... whatever "it" may be.

The American poet Henry Wadsworth Longfellow put it far more eloquently when he wrote, "Perseverance is a great element of success. If you only knock long enough and loud enough at the gate, you are sure to wake up somebody." This is one of those "golden oldies" — a truth that has been passed down through the centuries, and one that you must constantly remind yourself of, especially in the difficult times, to give yourself the reassurance and extra strength needed to push on. And there will be difficult times; there always are — for everyone. As the old adage goes, "If there were no shadows there'd be no sunshine." Another version of this saying, with the same meaning, is, "Behind every shadow there is always a light shining." Think about it.

Indeed, life is full of peaks and troughs — or, as some might put it, mountain-top and valley-floor experiences. It's the same for everyone, without exception. That's life. It is in the low times that our characters are built and refined. Winners know this but, even when on a low, winners don't look down: instead, they are always looking upwards, forwards, towards the high ground, where the view is so much better.

The famous 19th-century American author Oliver Wendell Holmes wrote, "The great thing in this world is not so much where we are, but in what direction we are heading." Ask yourself, overall, which direction you are heading in. The answer should be: upwards and onwards. And that's the key: no matter what happens, you must not give up hope; you must always remain optimistic, always be looking upwards. It's not easy. Success is never easy, which is why the rewards are so great for those who achieve it.

Staying on the theme of upwards and onwards, Joel Weldon tells an interesting and encouraging tale of persistence, preparation and growth, in the rise of the Moso bamboo. The Moso is a bamboo plant, native of the Far East. For up to five years after being planted, even in ideal conditions, there is no discernible development. The plant seemingly doesn't grow. Then, after several years of preparation, the Moso suddenly takes off and grows at up to two-and-a-half feet a day, every day, for up to six weeks, until it eventually reaches its full height of nearly 30 metres. Incredible growth, certainly. But that image doesn't quite portray the real truth. You see, for the first five years, the Moso bamboo was preparing itself in order to sustain its mighty rise to fame. For the first five years, the Moso laid down its foundations, with several miles of root system reaching far and wide into the earth.

Our success in life is often comparable. If we are to succeed, we have to lay down our foundations, and develop a root system of beliefs and experiences to sustain us and prepare us so that we can handle future growth.

Everyone is born with these seeds of greatness. Everyone is born to win. In fact, during the act of procreation itself, somewhere between 200 and 300 million seeds are released. You won! Out of all those millions, you were destined to win the race, and you did. You are, in fact, not one in a million, but one in over 200 million. You were born to win … so don't give up now.

Indeed, everyone is born to win. Like the Moso bamboo, we all have massive potential, but success in life depends upon our performance, not our potential. "Born to win" doesn't so much mean that we are born winners (even though we won the first and most important race). Rather, we are born *to* win, or with the will to win.

Winners, then, are not so much born that way as they are made that way. It's true that some people attract good fortune, but, as is often said, that is because "good luck is what happens when preparation meets opportunity". In the final analysis, success doesn't just happen, it has to be worked hard for and earned. Without exception, one of the attributes shared by all successful people is that of a dogged determination; that of perseverance and persistence. Winners know that "giving up is bound to fail but perseverance will prevail". Winners know that "to become is to overcome". Perseverance is most definitely the hardest option. The fact is, it's much easier to quit, which is why there are so very few successful people. Here are the famous and encouraging words of English-born poet Edgar Albert Guest (1881–1959), from his verse titled "Don't Quit":

> *When things go wrong, as they sometimes will,*
> *When the road you are trudging seems all uphill,*
> *When the funds are low and the debts are high,*
> *And you want to smile but you have to sigh,*
> *When care is pressing you down a bit,*
> *Rest if you must, but don't you quit!*
>
> *Life is queer with its twists and turns,*
> *As everyone of us sometimes learns,*
> *And many a failure turns about,*
> *When he might have won had he stuck it out;*
> *So don't give up, though the pace seems slow,*
> *You might succeed with another blow!*
>
> *Success is failure turned inside out,*
> *The silver tint in the clouds of doubt,*
> *And you never can tell how close you are,*
> *It may be near when it seems afar;*
> *So stick to the fight when you are hardest hit,*
> *It's when things go wrong that you mustn't quit!*

This verse has spoken to me many times over the years, especially the line, "Don't give up, though the pace seems slow, you might succeed with another blow!" Another one of my favourite quotes is from Thomas Edison. Speaking about persistence, he once said, "Many of life's failures are people who did not realise how close they were to success when they gave up."

Edison himself was a great man of persistence. Over the course of his lifetime, he patented over 1,000 inventions, one of the most famous being the electrical candescent light bulb. The story goes that it took Edison several years, and many thousands of experiments, before he finally discovered the successful formula that gave us the electric light that we know today. During his many experiments, Edison failed thousands of times, and, no doubt, often felt dejected. But Thomas Edison was a man who knew that persistence conquers resistance. He persevered, and eventually he succeeded.

Now, to prove the point that persistence works, I am going to ask you a simple mathematical question, which I want you to try and answer as quickly as you can. Ready? What is 6 × 6? I think it's a pretty safe assumption to say that you answered that question almost instantaneously. Why is that? The answer is that when you were at junior school you were taught your multiplication tables verbatim, each table in the form of a chant, until you knew the words off by heart. As the saying goes, "Repetition is the mother of learning."

The point I am trying to make is that knowing our multiplication tables — or the alphabet for that matter — isn't something that simply happens to us; rather, it is something that is learnt through persistent repetition over a period of time. It's another case of persistence conquering resistance.

Most children know this secret. They know that if they ask for something and the answer is no — in other words, if they encounter resistance — then if they keep asking and asking, they will, they hope, wear down the resistance (and not the tolerance) of their parents, and eventually get their own way.

Persistence is very powerful. Consider for a moment the following little rhyme, which demonstrates beautifully just how awesome this "power of persistence" can be:

> *Little drops of water and tiny grains of sand,*
> *Make the mighty ocean and the pleasant land.*

Many people half-heartedly seeking success are of/
more than one-day wonders. They're just heroes for today and
for tomorrow, because they don't fully understand that the on.
way to be consistent is by being persistent. Professional athletes
must train constantly and persistently if they are to be consistent
performers. It is all very well aiming for gold, having a mighty surge
of energy and then giving it everything you've got in an all-out
effort to win, but without the persistent training beforehand, without
preparation, any success will only be short-lived. As someone once
noted, "The only place where success comes before work is in a
dictionary." You see, success is not down to one single thing; instead,
it's a culmination of many little things and much effort. In the
words of Thomas Edison once again, "Genius [success] is 1 per cent
inspiration and 99 per cent perspiration."

With persistence there is a real power, and in the right venture
much can be accomplished. I should point out, however, that
persistence can be just as harmful as it is helpful. Like anything that
contains power, it can be used for bad as well as for good. For
example, I'm sure you can see that if a person is prone to
discouragement and has a persistently negative outlook to life, this
would have a harmful effect on their future. Another example of
how this same power can be, and has been, used for its negative
effect is the infamous so-called Chinese water torture. Here, water
was made to drip onto a victim's forehead to either drive them insane
or make them talk. Once again, we see that persistence conquers
resistance.

On the same note, consider for a moment that droplets of water,
persistently dripping over time, are powerful enough to bore through
solid rock. But on the other hand, a mad rush, or a torrent, of water
would simply pass over the rock. Sure enough, there's power in the
torrent, but not enough to bore through the resistance of solid rock.
The torrent is powerful, but only for a passing moment. After it
has gone, there is no trace of it left behind. It takes persistence to
conquer resistance. As the ancient Chinese philosopher Confucius
once said, "A journey of a thousand miles begins with one step."

The Bible is, to me, a great source of inspiration and wisdom, and it contains much on the subject of persistence, to help and encourage us. For example, in the book of 2 Chronicles 15:7 (though somewhat out of context here, the message remains the same), God spoke through the prophet Azariah, saying, "But as for you, be strong and do not give up, for your work will be rewarded." Another example is St Paul's Letter to the Galatians, where it says, "Let us not become weary in doing good, for at the proper time we will reap a harvest if we do not give up." (Galatians 6:9 — all Bible quotes are from the popular New International Version.)

History is full of the success stories of persistent people. Like Benjamin Franklin (1706–90), one of America's most persistently creative men. In his book *Poor Richard's Almanack*, Franklin wrote the following wise words: "Little strokes fell great oaks." What Franklin was saying is that mighty works can be accomplished with persistent and sustained effort.

Calvin Coolidge, the 30th President of the United States, was another persistent man. It was Coolidge who said:

> Nothing in the world can take the place of persistence. Talent will not — nothing is more common than unsuccessful men with talent. Genius will not — unrewarded genius is almost a proverb. Education will not — the world is full of educated failures. Persistence and determination alone are omnipotent.

Yet another great example of success through persistence is Sir Winston Churchill. In June 1940, when Britain was facing overwhelming odds during the Second World War, and with the imminent threat of invasion and defeat, Churchill rallied the troops with this speech and radio broadcast:

> We shall not flag or fail. We shall fight in France, we shall fight on the seas and oceans, we shall fight with growing confidence and growing strength, we shall defend our island, whatever the cost may be, we shall fight on the beaches, we shall fight on the landing

grounds, we shall fight in the fields and in the streets, we shall fight in the hills; we shall never surrender.

Finally, let me quote another very determined and persistent person, Lady Margaret Thatcher, who, in her Conservative Party conference speech of 1980, said, "U-turn if you want to. The lady's not for turning."

Let me finish off by leaving you with a little verse that I came across some years ago. I liked it so much that I adopted it into my own life and belief system. I would encourage you to do the same. The author remains unknown to me. The verse is titled "Always Finish". Here it is:

> *When a task is once begun,*
> *Leave it not until it's done,*
> *And be a labour great or small,*
> *Do it well or not at all.*

Well, by now you should have got the message loud and clear. To conclude, let me remind you to be on your guard so that you don't fall prey to discouragement. Remember, a quitter never wins and a winner never quits. So, don't be a hero for today and a zero for tomorrow. Don't be a one day-wonder — be consistent by being persistent. Stick with it, Go-getter. I'll write again soon.

Yours cordially,

Uncle Bob

CHAPTER TWO

Enthusiasm and Positive Mental Attitude

Dear Go-getter,

PERSISTENCE IS NOT all you will need to succeed in the game of life. You will also need to have enthusiasm and a healthy attitude. Both of these are particularly important — so much so that I'm going to dedicate this letter to those very subjects: the power of enthusiasm and a positive mental attitude.

First off, though, I'd like to encourage you to retain my letters and reread them at regular intervals, and especially during challenging times. We all need reassurance and encouragement from time to time, and, even when we already know something to be true, we still need to be reminded of it. As an example, when my wife and I were married, we both knew that we loved each other, and of course we told each other as much. Now, knowing that you love each other is something you don't easily forget. Nevertheless, we still need to tell each other, and often do, to reassure and encourage one another. The same applies to life in general. Even when we know something to be true, we still need to remind ourselves of the truth every now and again, so that we don't forget it. Hopefully, my letters will help to serve that purpose.

So, then, let's start by looking at enthusiasm. Enthusiasm is a beautiful word, originating from the Greek words *enthousiazein* (meaning possessed by God) and *entheos* (meaning God-inspired). Its literal translation, then, is "God in us". And the last four letters of enthusiasm, IASM, are an acronym for I Am Sold Myself. Having enthusiasm about something, whether it's a concept or a product, or even another person, means just that: I am sold myself, hook, line and sinker. With that kind of enthusiasm and belief comes a godly power that makes impossible things happen. As Jesus of Nazareth told us, "Everything is possible for him who believes." (Mark 9:23) Now, that enthuses me!

Let me tell you of another enthusiastic person: I call him Mr Bumble. Mr Bumble is a small toy bumblebee given to me by my son, Aaron, and I often carry him around in my briefcase (the toy, not Aaron) to remind me that everything really is possible for those who believe. Let me explain. The bumblebee is one of the most enthusiastic fellows around. During the summer months, the bee is one of the earliest creatures to rise in the morning and one of the last to bed at night. All day long, he remains focused on his objective: collecting nectar from flowers to make honey. Throughout the long summer days, bees can fly up to 1,600 kilometres a week, which is quite a feat when you consider that, on average, a bumblebee is only about two-and-a-half centimetres long.

The truly amazing fact, though, is that a bee shouldn't be able to fly at all. I have read that scientific evidence overwhelmingly points to the fact that a bumblebee shouldn't be able to fly. Its wings are a disproportionate size to its body — they're too small and too light. Its body is too round and fat and heavy. Its shape is not at all aerodynamic. The plain fact is, it should be impossible for a bumblebee to fly, never mind it being able to hover over a flower to collect nectar. So, how does our enthusiastic friend do it? How does he achieve the impossible? Well, to my thinking, and put simply, when God created the bumblebee, He forgot to tell him that he couldn't fly. In other words, the bee doesn't know any better.

Mr Bumble doesn't concentrate on all the reasons why he can't do it. He just gets on and does it — with enthusiasm. So, you see, this just goes to prove that "everything really is possible for those who believe".

There are many things in this world that we don't yet understand — and, indeed, many that will always remain unexplainable. However, more and more scientists, researchers, doctors, psychologists, businesspeople, athletes — you name it — are coming to realise and understand that the way we think determines the results we can achieve. Today, we no longer have to prove that high self-esteem and a Positive Mental Attitude (PMA) are prerequisites for success. This is now commonly held to be true, and there are numerous seminars and classes — not to mention books such as this one — that promote this, and teach people how to use their mental abilities for self-improvement.

Let me tell you about one of my own experiences using PMA. Some years ago, I was performing an advanced sales training course with a group of six salespeople. Throughout the week, my class, being very small in number, became quite friendly and familiar with each other, and I can remember sharing with them during the last morning session one of the routines that I used to perform when I was a salesman. I told them how I would psych myself up each morning before I started work. One of my routines was to toss a coin into the air, saying to myself, "Heads I make a sale today, tails I don't." At the same time, I would picture in my mind the heads side of a coin and I would will the coin, with every ounce of my being, to fall on heads. Most of the time, the coin did just that. Then my confidence and spirits would soar and, sure enough, my prophecy or prediction of making a sale would come to pass.

However, the coin would occasionally land on tails. Whenever this happened, I would dismiss the foolish, childish ritual as nothing more than superstitious nonsense, and I would become determined to break the spell and prove, once and for all, that my fate was not decided by the throw of a coin. As far as I can remember, this is something that I was never able to do, the reason being that when the coin landed on tails, what I saw subconsciously in my mind's eye was defeat. It wasn't until later in my career, after reading Dr Norman Vincent Peale's best-seller *The Power of Positive Thinking*, that I realised the folly of what I was doing and decided to quit this destructive habit. From then on, instead of wasting time and energy trying to determine the fall of a coin, I decided to concentrate my mind on seeing the customer buying my product, and willing a positive and worthwhile outcome. Needless to say, my performance went up dramatically as a result.

After relating this story to the group, one of them — a woman named Cathy — requested that I demonstrate this "power of positive thinking" by tossing a coin for each of them and predicting the outcome. I was then overwhelmed with similar requests from the others, who eventually closed me down with statements such as, "Go on, just for fun, it can't do any harm." It had been a good week, and that particular morning session had gone very well indeed. Everyone was highly motivated and enthusiastic, including myself, and so, throwing caution to the wind, I foolishly bowed to the pressure and agreed.

What started out as a jovial, light-hearted exercise to try and prove a point, suddenly became serious as I realised that I was being tested. As I have already said, I was brimming with confidence, but all I can say to explain what happened next is that I already knew, without any shadow of a doubt whatsoever, what the outcome would be. As I went around the table, I looked at each person in turn and simply said, "Heads." In my mind's eye, I saw the coin land on heads, and as I tossed it high into the air, I silently willed for it to be so. Six times I threw the coin in the air, six times I made the prophecy aloud and six times the coin landed on heads. The atmosphere amongst the group was electric. There was a hushed silence, and a reverence that could be both seen and felt. I was completely confident of the outcome of each throw, and I could tell that the others were secretly joining in with me. It wasn't only myself, but each of them was also willing and expecting the coin to fall on heads. Then Cathy, with a mischievous twinkle in her eyes, looked at me, and with a faint smile she commanded, rather than requested, "Again." Before I had time to properly think about it, the coin was in the air —

heads! "Again," was the only response from Cathy, the smile now gone — heads! "Again … again … again …" The rest of the group were mesmerised by what was happening, and, although no one spoke, I could tell that they, too, were expecting the coin to land on heads. Nine more times the coin was in the air, nine more times it fell on heads, and then I suddenly decided to stop.

Up until the ninth additional throw, I had been absolutely convinced of each outcome. There was an indescribable power that I had tapped into — I call it the "ABC factor" (Attitude, Belief and Conviction). What I had visualised, and internally verbalised, was actualised. It became a reality. However, on the ninth fall of the coin, the ABC factor died, as the thought occurred to me that this situation couldn't go on forever. Eventually it would give. It had to, it was logical. When doubt sets in, the ABC factor packs in, and therefore I knew that I had to do the same. Nevertheless, the point had been proven.

Some folk would put what happened down to chance, luck or coincidence. Of course, everyone is free to believe whatever they like, but for myself and many others, this is an example of the power of the mind. Later on, I sat down and reflected upon what had taken place, and I worked out the odds against what had happened. All in all, I tossed the coin 15 times (initially, once for each of the six salespeople, and then a further nine times for Cathy alone), and 15 times the coin landed on heads. The odds of this happening are 2 to the power of 15: that's a probability of 1 in 32,768. Some people say, "Seeing is believing," but I say it's the other way around: "Believing is seeing." You have to believe that whatever it is you want, can and will happen. Wondering whether or not it will work is doubting, and when this happens, try as you might, the desired results will not be forthcoming. In his best-selling book *Tough Times Never Last, But Tough People Do!*, Dr Robert H. Schuller writes, "Have faith in your faith — and doubt your doubts."

I intend to write further on this subject at a later date, but for now, suffice to say that this mental power is achieved through belief or faith, and never with doubt. There is also a very important universal truth about the use of this positive mental power: it only works when it is used for the good of mankind, for positive results, and never for greed, gambling or personal gain. I am convinced that the incident I just portrayed only worked because it was beneficial to the group at that particular time, in demonstrating to them the power of positive thought, a power that is yet to be wholly understood but nevertheless is able to be captured and harnessed for good purposes. After that original occurrence, I tried on several occasions when I was alone to repeat the process with a coin, but I always failed. I believe the reason for this is that I was only ever testing to see if I could make it work again. In other words, there was no worthwhile or positive purpose behind it.

There is another universal truth about the power of positive thinking: although with positive thinking we can achieve fantastic results, those results cannot be put down just to the thinking itself. It is not as if you can attract any single thing you desire just through positive thinking or a positive mental attitude. For example, I am a fairly good runner. I jog about three times a week, and I can sprint 100 metres in decent time, but I don't consider myself an athlete. I am fit, but I'll never be able to compete in the 100 metres at the Olympics. All the positive thinking in the world isn't going to turn back the hands of time and enable me to beat 20-year-old athletes, regardless of my attitude.

The way we think is important — very important — but success takes more than just positive thinking. It also requires positive action. Someone once said, "The greatest idea in the world won't work unless you do." And that's basically what I'm getting at. Success can only ever be achieved through hard work coupled with a positive attitude. The following is a story I once heard which perfectly demonstrates this.

There was once a young salesman who went to work for a company selling office stationery. After the initial week of training, the salesman was allocated his territory or sales area, but before he hit the road, so to speak, he was ushered into the office of the sales manager for some last-minute instructions and a pep talk. The sales manager told the salesman that the company had great hopes for him.

Furthermore, to get him started and give him some first-hand experience in the processing of an order, the sales manager was going to send him to an account nearby that the company had been doing business with for many years. The sales manager went on to say, "Now, this man I'm sending you to is a very difficult person. He can be stubborn, awkward and very obnoxious, but unfortunately that's just the way he is. We know from years of experience that if you hang in there, don't let him rile you or get at you, if you persist in a friendly manner and keep asking for the order, then eventually he'll give it to you. He always does."

With that, the new recruit, armed with a positive attitude and full of enthusiasm, set off down the street to make his first sales call and become initiated. Just as the sales manager had said, the customer was indeed very obstinate, but the new salesman did as he was told: he stuck it out and kept trying for the order. Sure enough, his enthusiasm, positive attitude and persistence paid off, and eventually he walked away with a very sizable order indeed.

Upon returning to the office, the new recruit began to process the order, and handed a copy of his sales report to the sales manager's secretary. Moments later, the sales manager bounded up to the salesman's desk, frantically waving the sales report in the air and exclaiming that the sizable order was, in fact, the largest single order ever written in the history of the company. The sales manager congratulated the salesman and asked how he did it. Somewhat taken aback, the salesman related how the customer had given him a really hard time, just as the sales manager had said he would, but that the salesman just let it all wash over his head. He remained positive and was expectant, and so kept plugging away for the order, which eventually came, just as the manager had said it always did.

The sales manager still seemed puzzled and looked again at the copy of the order. Then it was his turn to be taken aback. With a sudden gasp of astonishment, the sales manager blurted out, "My goodness, you went to see the wrong chap! For over 20 years we've been trying to find a way into this account, but we've never before been able to get so much as a look in. I'd given up on this fellow years ago."

Now, the young salesperson was full of enthusiasm and had a positive mental attitude, there is no doubt about that. But success was not determined, nor was the sale made, in front of the customer. Success was determined beforehand, in the mind of the salesman before he had even met the customer. The salesman (like Mr Bumble) didn't know any better, and so he had already decided that the customer would buy. When it comes to the profession of selling, the following phrase just about sums it up: "If you don't have a PMA when you meet your customer, then you'll be DOA (Dead On Arrival)."

In his book on body talk, or non-verbal communication, titled *The Secret Language of Success*, Dr David Lewis gives another example of someone with a winning attitude. A middle-aged company director, a positive and successful man, was carefully reversing his Rolls Royce into a narrow parking space, when a young man in a battered old Mini nipped into the gap. Locking his car, the Mini driver remarked with a sarcastic grin, "Sorry, Granddad. The world belongs to the young and quick." Without a word, the businessman continued reversing, pushing the Mini sideways onto the footpath. He then locked the Rolls and handed his business card to the horrified youth. "No doubt your insurance company will contact me," he remarked calmly. "And you're wrong, by the way. It belongs to the winners in life who are not frightened to go the extra yard."

Although I certainly do not condone arrogance, this somewhat amusing story does portray a winning attitude. Nevertheless, I would suggest that in real life, the businessman would have been a far bigger winner had he been humble enough to turn the other cheek and walk away. You see, life is like a boomerang, in that you always get back what you send out. If you send out arrogance, then guess what you'll get back in return?

Remaining positive all the time is anything but easy, which is another reason why successful people are always in the minority. The fact is, it is twice as hard to be positive as it is to be negative. To demonstrate my point, take a pen and draw a minus sign. How many strokes of your pen did that take? Now draw a plus sign. How many strokes of your pen did it take to do that? Like I said, it's twice as hard being positive! But the thing is, the benefits of a positive attitude are far more than twice as rewarding as a negative attitude.

Not so long ago, I was visiting a church where I heard a man preaching with much enthusiasm. After the service, I overheard someone say to him, "You're always so positive, is every day such a mountain-top experience for you?" The pastor replied, "Yep, every day — it's just that some days I'm on top of the mountain and other days the mountain is on top of me, but every day I have a mountain-top experience." That remark is often appropriate to those travelling on the pathway of self-improvement. We all have our ups and downs. No one is up 24 hours a day, seven days a week, 365 days a year — that much is fact. The difference, of course, lies in our attitude to that fact. Once again, the Bible gives us some sound advice. In Psalm 118 verse 24 we are told, "This is the day the Lord has made; let us rejoice and be glad in it." Anybody who doesn't agree with this comment and isn't glad about each new day should try missing one or two of them — then they would see just how precious each day really is. Life is too short to be negative.

As we are talking about attitude, what would you say if I told you that I know a secret that will guarantee 100 per cent success in whatever you do, 100 per cent of the time? Yes, you did read that right, 100 per cent guaranteed success in everything you do. Here's how: if you believe, if you have the attitude that you'll fail, then I guarantee you'll be right. If you believe that you'll fail, you will "succeed": you will, in fact, fail 100 per cent of the time. Henry Ford, founder of Ford Motor Company, once put it this way: "Whether you think you can or can't, either way you'll be right."

Let me give you another account of attitude at work. This is a story I heard about an international shoe-manufacturing company which had ambitions to expand into new markets. The abolition of apartheid in South Africa during the early 1990s presented new opportunities, so they decided to test the market. Initially, the company sent their most experienced salesperson, samples in hand, to get a feel for the market and sell what he could. Shortly after arriving in one of the townships, the experienced salesman sent a telegram back to the company saying, "No one here wears shoes STOP Market non-existent STOP Returning home asap." Now, although the company had great expectations, the fact is that a market has to exist before you can supply it.

However, the company didn't give up, and a couple of months later tried again. This time, though, instead of sending an experienced salesman the company sent a novice salesman who more than made up for his lack of experience with enthusiasm. The same thing happened: shortly after arriving, the company received another telegram. This one said, "No one here wears shoes STOP Market completely untouched STOP Send me everything you've got asap."

In the above example, the only difference between the first and second approach, between success and failure, was the difference in attitude. The first salesman had a negative attitude and saw only failure, whereas the second salesman had a positive attitude and saw only success. At the end of the day, we can control our own thoughts and therefore we can control and determine our attitude. The unknown author of the following verse certainly understood this principle:

The Man Who Thinks He Can

If you think you are beaten, you are,
If you think you dare not, you don't.
If you like to win, but think you can't,
It is almost certain you won't.

If you think you'll lose, you're lost,
For out in the world we find,
Success begins with a fellow's will,
It's all in the state of mind.

If you think you're outclassed, you are,
You've got to think high to rise,
You've got to be sure of yourself before
You can ever win a prize.

Life's battles don't always go
To the stronger or faster man,
But sooner or later, the man who wins,
Is the man who thinks he can!

All the real winners in life have a positive attitude. Look around and consider any of the successful people you know. One of the things you'll find they all have in common is enthusiasm for what they do, coupled with a positive mental attitude. Attitude speaks volumes about a person. I've read that when Abraham Lincoln was President of the United States, he once declined the advice of his associates to appoint a particular man for an important position within his government. His reason, he said, was that he didn't like the man's face. Lincoln's advisers apparently objected, saying, "How can a man be accountable for his face, the way he looks?" To this Lincoln replied, "Every man past the age of 40 is responsible for his face."

You see, Abraham Lincoln knew that you can tell a lot about a man's attitude by looking at his face. The man in question may very well have been the most appropriate man for the job, in terms of education or knowledge. However, it's not what you know, but what you do with what you know, that determines success. Zig Ziglar puts it this way: "It's our attitude not our aptitude that determines our altitude."

I'll leave you for now with this thought-provoking truth: There are three sorts of people in this world of ours — people who go out and make things happen, people who sit back and watch things happen and people who simply wonder what on earth did happen. Which sort are you?

Yours cordially,

Uncle Bob

CHAPTER THREE

Perception – Learning to Look and Listen

Dear Go-getter,

SOMETIMES IT'S HARD to be patient, particularly when you're full of energy, ambition and eagerness to storm ahead. We can all get frustrated at times, and often do when things aren't happening as fast as we would like them to. I know that in my own struggle for self-improvement, there have been, and continue to be, many lessons I wish I could simply have learnt and then moved on. Yet even now, I continually forget or fail to apply a new behaviour or skill, and all too often I have to pick myself up again and start over.

Nothing good, however, comes out of wallowing in self-pity at having failed — that much I do know. So, whenever I do fall short, I try to simply remind myself that practice makes perfect and then I start out again, not so much patient as persistent.

When it comes to learning life's lessons, I have often thought it would be wonderful to be able to take the great minds of the past and present and instantly transfer their knowledge, experiences and skills to myself, like copying information from a computer disk.

Or imagine if we could simply pick up some literature and, using our eyes like highly sophisticated computer scanners, be able to absorb every ounce of information in just a few seconds. Alas, such ideas are just a pipe-dream, an escape from reality. If obtaining experience and knowledge was as easy as that, then everyone would be successful in everything they ever did. (In fact, our brain does work very much in the way I've just described. But, as we are human beings and not machines, the transfer of information and programming often takes years, not seconds.) What it comes down to is this: if you don't put the effort in, you won't get the results out. As the old saying goes, "There's no such thing as a free lunch."

The only real way to learn and develop new skills is by watching, listening and then putting into practice what you have learnt. In this letter, I shall concentrate on those three areas.

Let me start, then, by asking you a question: Why do you suppose it is that man was created with two eyes and two ears, but only one mouth? Is it, perhaps, because we were meant to look and listen twice as much as we speak?

Listening takes special concentration. I remember, some time ago, watching some film clips on television. They were taken from a management seminar where one of the speakers was demonstrating how human beings have become poor listeners. To prove his point, the speaker asked the audience to participate in a little exercise. This is more or less what he asked them to do: "Would each member of the audience please raise their right hand into the air, and in a few seconds, when I say 'Now', put your hand down again and place it on to your right knee."

With that, the speaker raised his own hand, and the audience did likewise. He looked at his watch, nodding slightly, as if counting off the seconds. After about five or six seconds of silence, the speaker lowered his hand and touched his right knee. At the same time, he looked at the audience, raised his eyebrows and nodded for the audience to do the same. Almost everyone followed suit. Then, two seconds later, the speaker concluded the exercise by saying the word "Now".

Every one of the hundred or so people in the audience heard the instructions, but only about five or six of them actually listened to them. (The speaker had asked everyone to lower their hands when he said the word "Now", not when he nodded at them.) The point was well and truly made: we hear with our ears, but to listen we have to concentrate and use our minds as well. You see, hearing is a physical act, whereas listening is a mental act.

Now, let me move off at a tangent for a moment or two and ask you a completely unrelated question: How good is your English? I know that you can talk, and you can read and write. What I mean is, how good are you with pronunciation and grammar? Read the following statements aloud, and decide which of the two is the correct English:

The yolk of an egg is white.

or:

The yolk of an egg are white.

This little exercise was first given to me, or should I say tried out on me, many years ago by my grandmother, a wonderful lady who played a very significant role in my life and taught me many worthwhile lessons. The point of this particular lesson was to teach me the importance of listening and not simply hearing. I hope you got the answer right. If not, don't worry — neither did I the first time round, much to my grandmother's amusement. (The answer, just in case you missed it, is: Neither statement is correct. The yolk of an egg is yellow, not white.)

My grandmother then went on to remind me that King Solomon knew the wisdom of listening attentively. In the Book of Proverbs (18:13), he wrote, "He who answers without listening — that is his folly and his shame."

Recently, I read an extract taken from a book called *The Monday Connection*, written by William E. Diehl, who, I understand, is the president of a management-consulting firm in the United States. The excerpt reads as follows:

> Most of us are poor listeners. Since our mind moves
> forward faster than the words to which we are listening,

we are frequently preparing something to say when
we should be listening ... The world aches for good
listeners. Many doctors report that they daily see
patients who have nothing physically wrong with them.
They merely need someone to listen to them.

How true that statement is. It also reinforces another old saying,
"The world loves a good listener."

Remaining on the same theme, some time ago I attended a
seminar at which Rob Parsons, a lawyer and author, and the
executive director of CARE for the Family, spoke about the
importance of listening to our children and, particularly, to our
spouses. He suggested — rightly, in my opinion — that the reason
there are so many marriage breakdowns today is due to a lack of
communication and, specifically, a failure to listen to each other.
He went on to inform the audience, "Linguistic experts have
calculated that, on average, an adult person speaks around 14,000
words a day." In other words, each of us has around 14,000 words a
day that we need to communicate. Remember, this is an average
figure, so some people must speak a lot more than 14,000 words a
day and others considerably less.

Now, on the face of it, 14,000 words may seem a lot, but in reality
it isn't. To give you some idea, I am typing this letter to you on my
computer, which has a word-count facility. In this letter so far, up to
the word "facility" in the last sentence, there are 1,174 separate words,
which is about nine per cent of our average daily quota. And it has
probably only taken you about six minutes or so to read this far.

Parsons then went on to explain that if people thought about
the needs of others in those terms — that is, that they have around
14,000 words a day they need to communicate — the world would
be a far better place. Furthermore, there would likely be a lot less
failed marriages, and a lot less failed relationships between parents
and teenagers. Once again, the above example clearly shows the
importance of listening, and the truth behind the words, "The world
aches for good listeners."

Earlier, I quoted from the Book of Proverbs and the wisdom of
King Solomon. King Solomon also wrote, "Let the wise listen and

add to their learning." (Proverbs 1:5) Wise words indeed, especially for those in business. If we listen to our employees and managers, and especially to our customers, we can learn a great deal, particularly about how we can best satisfy their needs. And of course, in doing that, we will also satisfy our own needs. Here are some suggestions to help you increase your own effectiveness at listening:

1. Don't interrupt when another person is talking, and try not to assume what the other person is going to say — you just might be wrong.

2. Maintain eye contact. Not only does this help you to listen more attentively, it also shows the speaker that you're listening and taking an interest.

3. Listen out for an opportunity to nod your head in agreement, or occasionally raise your eyebrows, showing mild surprise. This will reassure the other person that you are listening, and also encourage them to keep talking.

4. It is impossible for a human being to think about two things at once. You must, therefore, give the person you are listening to the whole focus of your attention. In other words, don't allow your mind to wander. If you catch yourself drifting into another train of thought, pull yourself back again. People can tell when someone is not listening to them. If you get distracted, instead of pretending that you heard everything, it would be far better for you to say, "I'm sorry, I was distracted and missed that. Would you mind repeating what you just said?"

5. Remember to also listen for what is *not* being said. Look for non-verbal communications — body language.

6. Use the "echo" technique: every once in a while, repeat a word that the other person has said. This helps you to listen, and also invites the other person to elaborate. For example, if a client or prospect said, "There are a number of factors to be taken into consideration before we can make a decision," then you would simply turn around, raise your eyebrows and say, "Factors?" Or

if a potential customer says, "It costs too much," you would echo back, with a slightly puzzled expression, "Too much?"

In essence, what I'm talking about is developing your perception towards others. Allow me to explain and demonstrate further. First and foremost, the key to enhancing your perception comes down to one overriding factor: being aware that all too often we look at things without actually seeing what we are looking at. Here are a few examples:

Example 1. Look at the following statement and count how many times the letter F appears:

FINISHED FILES ARE THE RE-SULT OF YEARS OF SCIENTIF-IC STUDY COMBINED WITH THE EXPERIENCE OF MANY YEARS.

Most people count three Fs. If you only counted three, try again — but this time, look more carefully. (There are actually six Fs. For some reason, most people ignore the word "of", which appears three times.)

Example 2. Read the following:

HOW GOOD IS YOUR PERCEPTION? YOU COULD BE BE MISSING SOMETHING!

For example, the word "be" incorrectly occurs twice in the above statement.

Example 3. The German sociologist and psychiatrist Franz Muller-Lyer (1857–1916) discovered the following phenomenon, known as the Muller-Lyer illusion.

Look at the diagrams below and determine which line is longer, A or B:

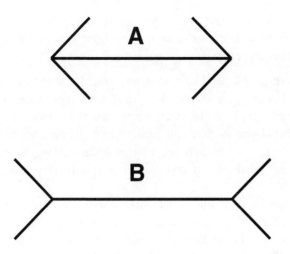

In fact, both lines are exactly the same length. This is an optical illusion: a line with arrowheads pointing inwards appears to be longer than a line of the same length, but with the arrowheads pointing outwards. (The proof lies in measuring the lines.)

The point I'm trying to make with the above examples is: be aware that things are not always as they might at first seem. Although I can't actually teach you how to perceive or view a particular situation, what I am endeavouring to do is make you aware that you can, and indeed must, look deeper. Instead of making a decision with a fleeting glance, train yourself to really look and you will often see a much different, and broader, picture.

Example 4. Here is a final example, which will, hopefully, drive the point home and make you more aware of the importance of using your perception. Your watch is something that you probably look at several times a day. Without looking at it right now, is the number six at the bottom of your watch the number "6", or is it the Roman numeral "VI"? Now, without reading any further, look at your watch and check to see whether you were right or wrong. It is amazing how many times we can look at something and still not actually see what we are looking at.

To conclude this exercise, let me ask you one final question: You have just looked at your watch — without looking again, do you know what the exact time is right now?

It doesn't matter how well or how badly you did with the above exercises. It is not my intention to try and trick you or catch you out. Rather, my emphasis is on trying to make you aware of the need to really listen, so that you hear what is being said, and to really look, so that you actually see what is often staring you in the face. In other words, I am trying to get you to develop your perception.

The human ear is made up of three parts: the outer ear, the middle ear and the inner ear. Now, just as the ear is made up of three parts, so we should listen to others as though we had three ears. It has been said that we should listen *to* what people are saying, listen for what they're *not* saying, and listen for what they are *trying* to say but can't put into words. Our ears also provide us with another vitally important function: namely, that of maintaining equilibrium or balance. So, if we apply the two-ears-and-one-mouth rule, if we listen twice as much as we speak, not only will we hear what is being said, but we will also maintain a healthy stability and balance in our conversations and our relationships.

There is another point I'd like to mention here. In business — especially in the profession of sales — it is extremely important to look and listen out for pertinent information from your prospects or customers. Search for unspoken wants or needs. As I've said before, it is very easy to become discouraged and accept defeat. If you are hearing objections, complaints and every reason under the sun why something is not possible or why a customer is not going to buy, then unless you are really focused on your objective, you will almost certainly fail. What you must do, then, is seek out and focus on the positive element, not the negative.

Allow me to demonstrate this point. The following passage is something I wrote some time ago for a sales training session. As you read it, I want you to ignore the word "negative", but count how many times you read the word "positive". (It is best to read it slowly, but to help you, every time the word "positive" appears, I've written it in bold type.)

Once upon a **positive** time, there was a negative young man and a negative young woman, who were so negative, they were **positive** that things were nearly always bad. Their job didn't help! The negative young man and the negative young woman both had negative jobs. They worked together as complaint officers for a **positive**, up-and-coming company that produces the film for photographic negatives. Practically all day long the negative couple would moan and groan about how bad things were. And of course, in doing so they just made matters worse. In fact, the manager was **positive** that the negative couple were having such a negative effect on the overall morale of the whole workforce, that even the employees who normally had a good **positive** attitude seemed to be catching the negative disease. The manager knew that he had to do something **positive** to lift morale, even if it meant firing the negative young man and the negative young woman!

The manager, though, was reluctant to do this. He didn't want to fire the negative couple because he was **positive** they both had the potential to do really well. It was obvious that something must be bothering the negative young couple, so much so that it was having a real negative effect upon them, both inside and outside of work. The manager decided to take the **positive** step of confronting the problem head on. So he went to see the negative couple, in order that they could discuss the problem and take **positive** steps to overcoming the negative atmosphere that was influencing everyone's attitudes.

The negative young man and the negative young woman told the manager that their problem was a personal one — stemming from the fact that they were having problems starting a family. They told the manager how their doctor was **positive** that they would both go out of their minds if they continued on this negative course, where things just seemed to keep moving from bad to worse. The doctor suggested that they needed to relax and escape to a more **positive** environment, he suggested they took a holiday. The negative young man and the negative young woman were **positive** that a vacation would do them the world of good but they were concerned that the manager wouldn't agree to them taking time off, due to their negative results at work lately ... The manager, however, upon hearing their plight was very understanding and indeed, he agreed to the negative couple taking two weeks leave but in a months time when he could arrange cover for them.

The negative young man and the negative young woman got to work straight away. They made a **positive** commitment and booked a romantic holiday in Venice, Italy. As the weeks passed by and the day of departure grew nearer they became more and more excited which in turn made them less negative and more **positive**. The funny thing is, the more **positive** they felt the more **positive** they became. It was a complete reversal. When they felt negative they acted negative, they attracted negative and became more and more negative. Now they were focusing on something **positive** they began to feel **positive** and act **positive** and they became more and more **positive**.

Well, as with all the best stories, this one has a happy ending ... The negative young man and the negative young woman had a fantastic vacation. After a wonderful time in a **positive** and relaxed atmosphere, the negative couple returned home feeling refreshed and really **positive**. A day or two later the negative young woman dropped into her local chemist for a pregnancy test and guess what? That result was **positive** too!

Now, the moral of this little tale is simply this; You must focus on the **positive** not the negative — that is, concentrate on the things you want not on the things you don't want!

The above passage is a little complicated to read, which means that you have to really concentrate on looking and listening. If you counted correctly, you will have noted that the word "positive" appears 24 times. Now I have another question for you. Without going back over the passage, how many times did you read the word "negative"? Hopefully, you'll have no idea, which is exactly what I wanted you to say. The reality is that there were far more "negatives" than there were "positives" — just as there are often more negatives than positives from a customer in a sales presentation. (The word "negative" actually appears 37 times.) My point, again, is this: you must not listen to negatives or focus on problems; rather, you must remain focused on the positive and search out solutions.

Develop your perception — and remember, the world loves a good listener (and a good looker, for that matter). Remember, also, that we have two eyes, two ears and one mouth for good reason.

Yours cordially,

Uncle Bob

CHAPTER FOUR

The Meaning of Life

Dear Go-getter,

FRESH BACK FROM our holiday in Barbados, my batteries recharged and my mind refocused, I am now sitting at my desk preparing this letter, with a twisted piece of drift-wood set down in front of me. Let me explain.

One day, I was walking along one of the many beautiful sandy beaches of the Caribbean and wading through the gentle surf of the Caribbean Sea, thinking about the future and deciding upon new goals. As I ambled along, deep in thought, I came across a piece of drift-wood bobbing up and down on the surface of the water. The next wave brought it ashore, so I picked it up and pondered upon how this beautiful piece of wood, which had been rounded and smoothed by the waves, had come to wash up on this beach.

As I contemplated what might have happened to this piece of drift-wood, I figured that it would make a good souvenir as well as an excellent prop or visual aid when I give talks about goal-setting. Consequently, I brought it home, and it is now lying in front of me as I write this letter to you. Let me expand upon my thoughts of that day and explain the relevance of this piece of drift-wood to the subject that I am writing to you about: finding purpose or direction in life and having goals to aim for.

For me, this piece of drift-wood represents a human life. At one time, the wood was obviously part of something much bigger. It has the marks of men upon it. A small hole, stained by rust, suggests there was once a screw or nail embedded there, and it is obvious that at one time the wood was cut and shaped for a purpose. Maybe it was once part of a yacht, or a small piece from a magnificent sailing ship. Maybe it was a plank or an old floorboard; maybe it was part of a fishing crate or an old tea chest. Who knows? One thing is for certain, though: my piece of drift-wood once had a purpose. It was made and crafted for a reason, it was designed to do something, somewhere, sometime, somehow.

What had happened to my piece of drift-wood I can only speculate, but for some reason it had become lost and ended up drifting about aimlessly with the tide. Maybe it had come down from the Gulf of Mexico, maybe it had travelled across the mighty Atlantic Ocean, or from a neighbouring Caribbean island. Whatever it was and wherever it had come from, the piece of wood was just drifting along aimlessly, seeking a sheltered harbour or a place to settle and call home. Perhaps, if the wood had been mindful, it would have been hoping that one day it would be appreciated again, possibly by someone looking for firewood, or maybe a beachcombing artist, or even an author and personal-development trainer, such as myself.

To me, this piece of drift-wood is representative of talented people who have somehow lost their way, people who don't quite know any more what they want in life or what it is that they want to do. Like my piece of drift-wood, they don't quite know where it is that they're heading for, so they simply plod along from one day to the next, hoping to find that sheltered harbour, a home or a place where they'll feel wanted, useful and appreciated.

I can certainly empathise with such people, because I know all too well what it feels like. I have been on that very same journey myself. The only way to escape from it is to discover (or rediscover) a meaningful purpose, and set goals to achieve that purpose. The American psychologist and philosopher William James (1842–1910) once made the following very profound statement: "The deepest principle in human nature is the craving to be appreciated." Let me paraphrase that by saying, "One of man's greatest desires is to find meaningful purpose in life and to know that his work is worthwhile."

Another philosopher once voiced this opinion about the life of man:

> Man is Nothing; but fat enough for seven bars of soap, iron enough for one medium-sized nail, sugar enough to fill seven cups of tea, lime enough to whitewash one chicken coop, phosphorous enough to tip 2,200 matches, magnesium enough for one dose of salts, potash enough to explode one toy crane, and sulphur enough to rid one dog of fleas.

Now, there has to be more to life than that, and, quite frankly, there is. Robert Byrne put it this way: "The purpose of life is a life of purpose." Without a purpose, life is meaningless, empty, a void. I believe that everyone upon the face of this earth has a purpose. There's a reason why we are here, a God-given plan, an objective, our own special place or niche. It is up to each individual to search it out and find it. Only then will a person find true happiness. Someone once remarked that happiness is not a destination but a journey. How true that is. Success and happiness are not found at the end of a long pilgrimage. Rather, once we have discovered our purpose, they are our companions along the way. It is only in discovering our purpose that we really begin our journey.

As I have already said, purpose is something we have to seek out. It is not something that is miraculously revealed to us, or something that we discover accidentally. Often, people have said to me that they don't have a purpose and they don't really know what it is that they want to do. What these people were really saying is that their purpose is to find a goal in life. My advice to such people is always the same: "Do what you love and love what you do." There is something that you really enjoy, something that you are good at, something you love to do. Whatever it is — a talent, a skill or some natural ability — it will be something that gives you pleasure, something of use to others, something with which you can serve your fellow man and something that you truly like to do. Your purpose will be something that naturally attracts you — to the extent that you would perform whatever it is for free, if you had to. Whatever it is, find it, because this is what you should be doing, what you were meant to do. Find your purpose and you'll find your destiny.

Don't be tempted to become a "Jack of all trades" — instead, concentrate on what you love to do and become a master of that. The following fable illustrates my point. Brer Rabbit, Brer Duck and Brer Squirrel enrolled in the school for animal welfare. Each animal was an expert in his own field of athletics: Brer Rabbit at running, Brer Duck at swimming and Brer Squirrel at climbing. However, although each excelled in his own field, they all achieved very poor results in the other events. It was felt that they needed to put in extra time on the events that there weren't particularly good at. So, Brer Rabbit had to cut back on his running and instead concentrate his efforts on swimming and climbing. Eventually, he improved, but in doing so, he had become just an average runner. Brer Duck, instead of swimming, practised full-time his running and climbing skills. He, too, improved a little, but in the end his webbed feet were so badly torn by running along stony pathways and climbing rough tree bark that he could no longer swim properly. And as for Brer Squirrel, well, he spent so much time swimming and running that his claws were worn away to nothing. In the end, he could no longer grip the trees trunks and he stopped climbing altogether. And the moral of this story? Concentrate on what you do best and become an expert at it.

To move from where you are now to the place where you want to be, you must make plans to travel. You must set goals. John Ruskin (1819–1900), the famous English art critic and social reformer, once said, "When love and skill work together, expect a masterpiece." When your abilities work in harmony with your purpose, you can expect the same.

Most people in life want happiness, good health, financial security and so on, but most people are not serious enough to plan how to get what they want. Instead, they wander aimlessly around, like a piece of drift-wood, waiting for success to come to them or waiting for purpose to reveal itself. In the real world, if you fail to plan then, really, you plan to fail. Seneca (4BC–65AD), the Roman philosopher, statesman and dramatist, once wrote, "Our plans miscarry because they have no aim. When a man does not know what harbour he is making for, no wind is the right wind." In this regard, not much has changed in the 2,000 years since Seneca wrote those words. On my travels over the years, I have met and known many talented people who have never really added up to anything. Why is that? The answer, unfortunately, is that they have no real plans. Sure, they have an idea of where they want to be, but they have no real idea of how to get there or how long it will take.

Imagine, for a moment, a doctor about to perform major surgery on a patient, but without first of all taking x-rays or planning the operation. What would you think about the doctor's competence or his will to succeed if his attitude was one of, "Well, let's just open her up, see what we've got in there and take it as it comes"? Or imagine a construction worker undertaking the task of building a magnificent house, but without any plans or drawings to follow. Or how about a person who is set upon driving across Europe, but without a map. Instead, the driver says to himself, "If I just keep heading south then I won't get lost and I'll eventually arrive at my destination." Finally, imagine meeting a person who was eager and keen to succeed in life, but who had no goals and no real idea or plan of how they were going to achieve their purpose. What would you think about that person's competence or will to succeed?

I have to admit that there have been many times when I have lacked direction and understanding and not known what to do, which is why I feel qualified to write on this subject. My advice, then, is this: make plans and take action. Don't wait for opportunity to knock on your door, because that just doesn't happen. Waiting for opportunity to come to you is like standing in the middle of a cricket pitch with your hands cupped together, waiting to catch the ball. It just doesn't happen. Opportunity doesn't knock on doors, it hides behind them. If you are lost and not sure what to do, try pushing a few doors, and, if one opens for you, take a look inside. (You can always step out again.) I have found from experience that the longer you look and the harder you seek, the more worthwhile and valuable is the treasure when you do eventually find it.

Action, then, means doing; turning your good intentions into ACts in moTION. Remember what I said in a previous letter: there are three kinds of people in this world — people who make things happen, people who watch things happen and people who wonder what on earth did happen. The people who make things happen are the ones who have a plan, a strategy, a method for achieving success and self-improvement through goal-setting. Now, I can show you how to do this. I can show you how to set goals and how to achieve them, but I can't actually set or achieve them for you. That is something you must do for yourself. The ironic thing about goal-setting is that many people understand the principles and importance of it, yet few people actually do it. This is another reason why there are so few successful individuals in the world. The fact is, most people spend more time planning a two-week holiday than they do planning their lives and career aspirations. Why is it that there is such a reluctance for individuals to set goals and plan properly for the future? The answer lies in:

1. The amount of effort involved in working to achieve the goal; and
2. The fear of failure.

Unfortunately, there are far too many people wasting their time looking for the quick fix or a secret formula that will give them instant success. These are the sort of people who walk down the street imagining that they might find an envelope full of money just lying in the gutter. This, of course, is nothing more than wishful thinking. It is only when a person realises that life is in the doing and not the waiting, will things start to happen. Someone once said, "There are only two ways to climb an oak tree. You can climb it or you can sit on an acorn." In other words, you are in control of your own destiny. You can either do something about it — plan and set goals — or you can sit around and wait for life to pass you by.

Sometimes, when I conduct a training class or participate at seminars, I use a tape measure or else draw a line similar to the one shown below, to demonstrate the importance of planning, goal-setting and getting into action. I call it "The Lifeline".

Birth ++ Death

Follow along with me for a moment. This "Lifeline" represents a person's life, with each mark denoting one year. What I would like you to do is draw an "X" to indicate where on the line of life you think you might be at present. Once you have done this, take your pen or pencil and scribble out all the marks on the line to the left of your "X" back to the word "Birth". This, then, represents that part of your life that is now over and done with. There is no going back, and there's nothing you can do about it. It is already finished and gone forever.

This is a very profound exercise, and in a teaching environment it creates a solemn air as many people realise, sometimes for the very first time, just how much of their life has already gone by. As people literally see their life before their eyes, I emphasise the point that what's done is done, there is no point dwelling on it. What is important now is the future, not the past. And the future — indeed, your future — begins right now. The fact is that nobody knows how long they have left, so doesn't it make sense to make the best use of your unused time before it runs out?

It takes a special strength of character and discipline to set goals, to plan your work and then work your plan, but the results far outweigh the price tag. There is a wise old proverb that states, "Discipline weighs ounces but regret weighs tons." Think about it. A lot of people reach a certain age and then live out the rest of their lives regretting all the things they wish they had done, but hadn't. And then, there are a lot of others who live each day in the dream world of, "One day, I'll do this," or "One day, I'll do that." Decide right now to never become one of those people. Instead, discipline yourself to set worthwhile and achievable goals and then jump into action. Don't waste any more time, don't delay any longer, just do it, do it right, and do it right now.

If you need further persuasion of the effects of goal-setting, I have read about a study undertaken in 1953 at Yale University in

Connecticut, in the United States. The study — to establish the effects of goal-setting — was apparently performed on senior-year students just prior to their graduation. It ascertained that 87 per cent of the pupils had not carried out any form of goal-setting exercise at all. Ten per cent of the pupils had a general idea of what they wanted, and had made some attempt to set themselves goals. But only 3 per cent of the graduating students had actually sat down and created a plan of action, a goal-setting agenda. But the story doesn't end there. In 1973, some 20 years later, the study was finally concluded and the results published. The study found that over the interim 20-year period, the 3 per cent of students who had set themselves goals had achieved far more, in terms of both professional and financial attainments, than all the other 97 per cent put together. So, you see, goal-setting really does work.

Over the years, much has been written on the art of goal-setting, but, at the end of the day, there is no one method that is any better than another. However, having said that, I would like to give you my own simplified version of an effective goal-setting procedure. First, though, I want you to understand that success is determined by discipline, drive and determination, not by some fancy procedure. There is no magic formula. At the end of the day, the only method that works is vision coupled with hard work. But before we look at the principles of goal-setting, let me share with you another verse, which is most pertinent to the topic under discussion. This verse, once again, was penned by Edgar Albert Guest.

It Couldn't Be Done

Somebody said that it couldn't be done,
But he with a chuckle replied
That "maybe it couldn't," but he would be one
Who wouldn't say so till he'd tried.

So he buckled right in with the trace of a grin
On his face. If he worried he hid it.
He started to sing as he tackled the thing
That couldn't be done, and he did it.

Somebody scoffed: "Oh you'll never do that;
At least no one has ever done it";
But he took off his coat and he took off his hat,
And the first thing we knew he'd begun it.

With a lift of his chin and a bit of a grin,
Without any doubting or quiddit,
He started to sing as he tackled the thing
That couldn't be done, and he did it.

There are thousands to tell you it cannot be done,
There are thousands to prophesy failure;
There are thousands to point out to you one by one,
The dangers that await to assail you.

But just buckle in with a bit of a grin,
Just take off your coat and go to it;
Just start to sing as you tackle the thing
That "cannot be done," and you'll do it.

Let us now look, then, at the principles involved in setting and achieving goals. When it comes to goal-setting, I always write the word "goal" as "goall", to remind me to "go all" the way. Simply committing a goal to paper and then doing nothing more about it means that the goal is not worth the paper it is written on. As Benjamin Franklin once wrote, "Well done is better than well said." Appreciate, then, that there are no magic happenings when we commit a goal to paper, but commit it to paper we must. (When people are starting from scratch, I always suggest that it would be a good idea to, firstly, create their own list of desirables, or a "wish list" of things that they would really like to happen, or that they would like to own or achieve.)

These, then, are the 10 steps:

1. *Write your goals on paper*

   This gives the goal substance and clarity, and makes it easy to remember. Frankly, I believe that if you can't be bothered to write them down then you won't be bothered to achieve them. Putting a goal into black and white is like making a contract, a promise or an agreement with yourself. Your first commitment, then, should be to commit it to paper.

2. *KISS it – Keep It Short and Simple*

   Don't write pages of script; instead, keep things as simple as possible. That way, a goal is easy to see, read and remember.

3. *A goal should be a genuine desire*

   A goal should be something you will work for, something that's important to you. The story is told of a youth who went to visit a wise old man to discover the secret of success and wisdom. The wise old man instructed the youth to follow him, and then, taking him by the hand, he led him to a nearby lake. The old man didn't stop at the water's edge. Instead, he waded into the water, still holding the youth's hand. Deeper and deeper went the old man, until the boy's head was submerged below the surface. Then, a few seconds later, the old man turned around and led the grateful youth back to the water's edge, whereupon the wise old man asked, "When you were under the water, what was it that you desired more than anything else in the whole world?" The youth responded without any hesitation, "I wanted air to breathe!" The wise old man then said, "In order for you to find success and wisdom, you must want it as badly as you wanted the air when you were under the water." The same principle applies to goal-setting: a goal must be passionately desired for it to be achieved.

4. *Be realistic, but at the same time optimistic*

   A goal should push you, it should be something that you have to strive for, otherwise you won't try very hard or take the goal seriously. Remember, success is determined by discipline, drive and determination.

5. *Be specific*

   Be absolutely clear as to what you must do to achieve results, and how and when you must do it. Reduce the goal to manageable units. Whatever it is — weight loss, a certain amount of money, a sales target — break the overall goal down to manageable units. For example, if the goal is to lose ten kilos in weight, don't focus on the ten kilos; instead, break it down to two kilos a week for five weeks. That is specific and manageable. Remember this: "By the mile it's a trial, by the yard it's hard, but by the inch it's a cinch." So, be specific in whatever it is you would like to achieve or attain, and then break it down into small, manageable and achievable parts.

6. *Get to work*

Actions speak louder than words, and now is the time to turn those good intentions into action — ACts in moTION. No doubt, you will be familiar with the saying, "If the job's worth doing, it's worth doing well." This saying can also be paraphrased to say, "If a goal is worth setting, then it's worth achieving as well." So, this is a vital step, and one where a lot of goals are both won and lost.

7. *Monitor, review and adjust if necessary*

Understand that the overall aim of goal-setting is to hit a target or achieve an end result. This has often been compared to a surface-to-air missile, which locks onto the target and doesn't let go. The missile never runs in a perfectly straight path; rather, it constantly deviates from a true course due to the effects of atmospheric pressure, weather conditions and the movement of the missile launcher during firing. However, the missile has an onboard computer — an in-built homing device which continually monitors, reviews and makes any necessary adjustments to the flight path until such time as the target is reached.

It is the same with striving to achieve goals. If you monitor and review your performance, you will be able to work out how you are doing and make any necessary adjustments, either to the size of the goal or the time span for attaining it. The idea here is not to give you an escape hatch, but to encourage and inspire you onwards. If you know where you are, then you know what you have to do to get where you want to go. If you find that you are way in front of yourself, don't sit back and relax. Instead, change the target, make it bigger. (Remember, be realistic but *optimistic*.) On the other hand, if you figure that things aren't working out as well as you would like, don't quit, don't throw in the towel; simply readjust the goal. Any achievement is better than no achievement at all.

8. *Keep them to yourself*

    You should keep your personal goals private, because there will always be people who will try to discourage you. Don't give them the chance to pull you down with their sinking ship. The kind of people who try to ridicule others or pull them down do so because they are envious and feel threatened by the other person's potential success. When they listen to other people's ambitions and see others striving for success and self-improvement, it only reveals their own inadequacies and shortcomings. Truth be told, what these people try to do is not so much pull you down as pull themselves up. But, of course, the quickest and easiest way of getting to the same level as you is by pulling you down to their own level. Don't permit that to happen. Keep your goals to yourself and you won't get dragged down into the quicksand with the unfortunates.

9. *Set different ranges of goals*

    Long-term goals should not be too specific. The fact is, the further away something is, the less significant it seems. The important thing is to have an overall objective in mind: to know where you want to be a few years down the track. All your other goals should then be pointing you in this direction. Medium-term goals are those things you set out to achieve within the next 12 months or so. (I have about a dozen of these.) By far the most important, though, are the short-term or immediate-term goals, set weekly or even daily. A daily "things to do" list is a marvellous goal-achieving tool. Ticking off each item on your list when it has been done produces a sense of accomplishment which will both inspire you and motivate you to push on towards your longer-term goals.

10. *Concentrate on smashing through them*

When professional athletes approach the finishing line, they don't slow down; instead, they search their reserves for that extra push and then race flat-out for the line. In fact, professional runners don't stop when they reach the finishing line — they can't, because they are running so fast they need time to slow down afterwards. Similarly, a martial arts expert doesn't focus on the object he is going to break; instead, he focuses past it. So, when it comes to striving towards a goal, don't stop at the finishing line. Instead, set yourself a new target, a new finishing line — a new goal to replace the one you just "lost" by winning it.

Yours cordially,

Uncle Bob

CHAPTER FIVE

Learn More and Earn More

Dear Go-getter,

SOONER OR LATER, you will be called upon to give a public speech of some kind. Indeed, possibly you have already. Public speaking is today ranked as one of the things people are most apprehensive about. This is mainly caused by a lack of confidence, or, more aptly, the fear of making a fool of oneself. And yet, the very fact that you are called upon to speak in the first place means, quite frankly, that you must be considered worth listening to. In the latter part of this letter, I shall offer you my own thoughts and advice on the subject.

First of all, though, I want to encourage you to keep learning. By that, I mean: never stop educating yourself. The saying "Life is a learning experience" (meaning that we learn through our mistakes) is very true. However, I want to expound here upon the issue of learning through educating yourself rather than simply learning through your mistakes. Now, I am not suggesting for one moment that you have to be a highly educated scholar in order to succeed or get on in life. But what I am suggesting is that if you genuinely desire success and self-improvement, then you must become an expert and continually learn all you can in your chosen field or subject. It was the English philosopher Francis Bacon (1561–1626) who coined the now-popular phrase, "Knowledge is power." I agree that knowledge is power — but only, of course, if you put that knowledge to work for you.

Many individuals give up on education as soon as they finish school and move into the workplace. Now, in itself, there is nothing wrong with that. In fact, some of the happiest and hardest-working people I know are not that highly educated. But there are many others in the marketplace who have simply given up on learning. By that, I mean people who can't be bothered to pay the cost — that is, to put in the effort necessary to further educate themselves.

Similarly, there are many others who have a know-it-all attitude and think that they don't need to learn or develop any further in their chosen field. Such people normally disguise this deficiency and their lack of zeal — or "get up and go" — with the attitude of, "If you want to get on in life, it's not what you know but who you know that counts." Whilst I agree with this sentiment to a certain degree, my own attitude is one of, "If you learn more you earn more."

Let me encourage you, then, to keep learning, and keep reading, researching and studying whatever it is that you have an interest in. Never stop educating yourself. At the end of the day, the only way to reach the top is through much learning and a lot of effort or hard work. And then, once you achieve your goal, the only way to maintain and retain your position is through continued learning, practising and improving. This is similar to the situation of a professional athlete: the only way an athlete can remain fit and maintain a winning performance is through continual training. The same applies in the quest for success and self-improvement. You must keep training, you must continue learning and feeding your mind. Don't ever stop. This old proverb sums it up very well indeed: "When you're green you're still growing, but when you stop you start to rot." Don't ever stop growing. Don't ever stop learning, because as soon as you do, you will start to rot.

Let me put it this way: this road that we are travelling, this life-long journey to success and self-improvement, is comparable to travelling in a hot-air balloon. To continue your journey, you must constantly ascend to greater heights by applying the necessary fuel — turning on the gas and heating up the air inside the balloon. (You must keep learning, you must keep feeding your mind with the necessary fuel.) It's okay to shut off the fuel supply every now and again, because your hot-air balloon will happily hang in suspension, for a time at least, while it rides along with the wind and air currents. In fact, your balloon is designed to do just that: allow you to keep turning the fuel supply on and off. Besides which, you were created to — and, indeed, you are supposed to — have a rest and enjoy the view every once in a while, otherwise the trip wouldn't be at all enjoyable or worthwhile.

However, you can't afford to sit back for too long, because if you don't reapply the fuel, your hot-air balloon will soon start to cool down and, inevitably, you will start to descend. Many people travelling on this journey don't recognise their own descent until it's too late to stop it. They become so comfortable with their position that, instead of concentrating on staying afloat and continuing to rise, they get carried away with watching the view, and become inactive for far too long. Before they realise what is happening, their descent is out of control and then, no matter how hard they fight it, they eventually come back down to earth with a bump. If this happens, the balloonist has to start all over again from the beginning. (Or else they simply give up and call it a day.)

I share this analogy with you because "forewarned is forearmed". By this, I mean that being warned in advance of the potential danger allows you to prepare yourself, and arm yourself against it. Remember, prevention is better than cure. So, keep fuelling the fire, keep reading, seeking out information and learning, and never sit back for too long.

Remaining on the same theme, a while ago I came across this beautiful little phrase in my dictionary: "semper paratus". This is Latin for "always prepared". What a wonderful motto or guiding principle this Latin phrase makes. Semper paratus — always prepared: to do whatever it takes, to go the extra mile, to continue to learn and rise to greater heights and to never let up. I would like to encourage you to adopt semper paratus as your own personal motto, and I urge you to continue reading and learning as much as you can, so that you will "always be prepared".

"Reading is to the mind what exercise is to the body." Those wise words were written by Sir Richard Steele, the British essayist and dramatist (1672–1729). It can be said, then, that reading is mental exercise for the mind. And the human mind is like a magnet: it always attracts that which dominates our thinking. So, reading business, motivational and self-help books or listening to audio programmes and the like not only teaches you a great deal, it also affects your thinking. Your mind will be dominated with powerful, creative and positive thoughts obtained through your learning and this will have the magnetic effect of attracting whatever it is you are thinking about. (I will expand upon this further in a future letter.) Naturally, the opposite also applies, so being careful about what you actually read is obviously very important.

Often, when I speak on the subject of learning, people complain or make excuses about having a lack of time to study or read and learn new material or skills. Of course, I understand and appreciate that in today's fast-paced society there are many demands put on our time. But the thing is, some people are just better than others at managing their time. At the end of the day, finding the time — or should I say managing time effectively — is simply a matter of priority. Each of us is allocated the same amount of time each day and, for the most part, each of us decides how we will spend that time. Whether we realise it or not, we all prioritise the use of our own time, and sometimes people simply get their priorities wrong.

Now, here is an idea worthy of your consideration. A day consists of 24 hours, which is made up of 1,440 minutes. If you spend just 1 per cent of your time each day (to round it up, that's just 15 minutes a day) reading non-fiction material and learning new skills, then over the course of a year you will have invested over 91 hours in study time. If you will commit yourself to doing this — dedicating 1 per cent of each day to learning; that is, 15 minutes a day, day in day out — then I guarantee that you will achieve amazing results. Once again, it all comes down to discipline, drive and determination. There is no easy route.

Occasionally, people tell me that they are just so busy they could never find an extra 15 minutes each day. This is always an excuse — always. Of course, I can't make anyone do something that they don't really want to do — but, then again, that doesn't stop me from trying. Mostly, I answer these people by asking a few questions, such as:

♦ How long does it take you to drive to and from work each day? Did you know that there are some excellent audio-cassette programmes on the market? Why not turn drive-time into prime-time?

♦ How much time do you spend in front of the TV each evening? Why not switch off and "switch on" instead?

♦ How about setting your alarm clock to go off 15 minutes earlier each morning?

Finding the time is simply a matter of making priorities. If something is important to us, we will find the time to do it. And if it's not that important to us, we will either ignore it or make up excuses not to do it. This reminds me of the time when a sales manager in a company that I was doing some work for invited me and my wife to join him for dinner at his home. At the time, I wasn't overly impressed with this idea, as I didn't particularly agree with some of this man's views and work ethics. I politely declined his kind invitation, saying something along the lines of, "I'm terribly sorry, but I'm just far too busy at the moment. I've just got so much on and I'm afraid I already have other plans. In fact, I'm booked solid for the next week or so, but thank you anyway." When I got home that evening and explained to my wife what had happened, I came up with every excuse under the sun as to why it would have been impossible for me to accept this fellow's invitation. My wife, wise as she is, simply said, "You mean, those other things (excuses) have a higher priority for your time?"

Like I said, if it is important to us we'll find the time to do it, and if it's not that important to us, we will either ignore it or make up excuses not to do it. (Incidentally, I went back to this man and accepted his offer and, wouldn't you know it, we ended up having a wonderful evening. I just needed to get my priorities right.)

The cost involved in learning is, obviously, an investment of time. But it also usually involves a little money. On this point, let me assure you that every penny spent is worth a pound. Benjamin Franklin was a man who agreed with this philosophy. He once wrote, "Empty the pennies from your purse into your mind and your mind will fill your purse with pennies." To master the art of learning a particular skill — or anything, for that matter — involves a process which has been referred to as the "four levels of competence". These levels, or steps, are shown below.

1. *Unconscious incompetence*

   At first, while we are learning some new skill, we are not aware that we're incompetent at performing that new skill. We might try our hand at something and figure that we did okay, but it is not until we reach the next level of awareness that we realise differently.

2. *Conscious incompetence*

   As we become more experienced and learn more, we then become aware of the fact that our efforts are inadequate. We become conscious of the fact that we are, indeed, incompetent. This then leads us to the next step.

3. *Conscious competence*

   As we then persevere in our efforts to improve, we eventually become aware of our development and growing proficiency. We become conscious that we are now competent at what we are doing. And then, finally, we move up to the top step.

4. *Unconscious competence*

   After much practice, we become so conversant in our new skill or ability that it becomes second nature to us. We can then perform whatever it is well enough to be able to do it without conscious thought. We become, therefore, unconsciously competent.

Life really is a learning experience. Often, we make mistakes or errors of judgement, but, as someone once said, "A man who never makes mistakes never makes anything." One thing we must not do, however, is dwell on our mistakes. Rather, we should learn from them and then put these lessons into practice. I can remember, as a young man, working as a commission-only salesman in a company that endorsed unethical, high-pressure selling techniques. I have to admit, being young, hungry for success, ambitious for recognition and eager to impress my peers, I made a gross error of judgement. I went along with the crowd and I employed more than one or two unethical practices to sell more of a product than was necessary. It wasn't until I left that company to go it alone that I came to see and fully realise the error of my ways.

From then on, I amended my methods and this, I must say, resulted in far more success than I had previously enjoyed. At the same time, I also decided to make it my lifetime goal to teach others to "tell it straight and sell it straight". Now my philosophy in life is this: "Life is like a boomerang, you always get back what you send out." Send out selfishness, greed and wrong-doings and that's what you will get back in return. On the other hand, send out goodness, concern for others and a willingness to serve, and you will get the same good things coming back to you. Yes, life really is a learning experience. Often, it is only after we do something wrong that we then learn how to do it right.

It's the same with public speaking — that, too, is a learning experience. Nowadays, there are more and more speaking clubs, such as Toastmasters, offering practical advice and first-hand experience in the art of oratory. (You can find your nearest Toastmasters club through your local library or on the Internet.) Alternatively, there are plenty of excellent books, audio cassettes and video programmes, readily available from any library or book store. One of the things that I did to improve my own impact and delivery at speaking venues, and which I can highly recommend, was to learn sign language. Now, I know that at first this might sound like a strange idea, but, let me tell you, the lessons I have learnt have been invaluable. Sign language is, really, the art of public speaking without actually speaking. Learning a new language that consists only of signs, gestures, facial expressions and body language has had an enormous effect on my own public-speaking ability and confidence. Now, not only can I communicate with deaf people (albeit somewhat basically — the initial Stage 1 course takes 30 weeks), but it was also great fun to learn and has been a real asset in my own speaking career.

As I have already said, there have been many books written about the art of public speaking and body language, and I have no intention of turning this letter into another such manual. (Two books that I can highly recommend are *The Secret Language of Success* by Dr David Lewis and *Success Secrets of the Motivational Superstars* by Michael Jeffreys.) In offering my own advice, I think the best approach is for me to list some tips and important points, in the form of a summary. So, here goes:

1. Of course, planning your speech is obviously very important. Find out as much as you can about your audience and direct your speech *to* them, rather than *at* them. In other words, tell them what they want to hear. Write your speech out and keep polishing it until you are relatively happy with it. I say "relatively happy" because you will never be 100 per cent happy with it — at least, I have never met anyone who was 100 per cent happy with what they had written. Of course, there will always be room for improvement, but remember, your aim is to deliver a speech, not write a best-seller.

2. Once you have written your speech out, practise your delivery aloud and in front of a mirror. Don't try to learn the speech off by heart, because, come the big day, you will put yourself under so much pressure to perform and remember everything that you could very easily crack under the strain or go to pieces. Unless you intend to actually read the speech verbatim, my advice is to practise and learn it as best you can, and then make a very simple summary on paper. When I speak, I often use notes or a short list of one-liners to remind and guide me.

3. Visualise yourself giving a good speech, and use self-talk and affirmations to muster confidence. Remember, the mind is like a magnet, inasmuch as it always attracts that which dominates our thinking. So, think positive thoughts, see yourself succeeding, use confident self-talk and dominate your mind with whatever it is that you would like to attract to yourself.

4. Some humorist, discussing the subject of public speaking, once said, "If you haven't struck oil within the first five minutes, stop boring." To stop this situation from arising, always try to open with a bang and close with a bang. Opening your speech in a powerful way grabs your audience's attention from the start. Closing in a similar fashion will leave a lasting impression and help the audience to remember your message.

5. Following on from the above, a good speech has a beginning, a middle and an end. It is also good practice to begin your speech by informing the audience what it is you're going to talk about, then go ahead and tell them, and, finally, recap by telling them what you've just told them.

6. Smile a lot. Someone once noted, "A smile is such a powerful tool; you can even break ice with it." One of the best-received speeches I have ever made was in St Petersburg, in Russia, a few years ago. I had no alternative but to smile a lot — and I do mean a lot. Let me explain. I was appointed by a Swedish investment company to speak and extend my sales training to their Russian employees. This all had to be done through an interpreter, which was no mean feat, especially as I can talk a lot and can often get excited when I'm doing so. I would, literally, say a sentence, then have to stop and wait for the interpreter to translate before I could say the next sentence. The interpreter, a young lady by the name of Tanya Blinova, was extremely quick and professional, but between sentences there was absolutely nothing that I could do except smile away for all I was worth. I felt like the Cheshire cat from Alice in Wonderland! In passing, I might add that, in general, Russian people are hungry for self-improvement. The representatives hung off my every word and

made me feel like a million dollars. Needless to say, I thoroughly enjoyed the experience.

7. Make your speech as personal as you can by making fleeting eye contact with as many people as possible. This keeps your audience involved in the speech. Although each person understands that you're addressing the crowd, if you keep catching their eye, they will feel as though you are talking directly to them.

8. Try to move around as much as possible, if not with your whole person then at least with your hands, gestures and facial expressions. Your movement keeps the flow going, it makes the speech active and visual and causes the audience to follow you and listen more carefully.

9. Following on from the above, use visual aids, humour, voice inflection, quotes, examples and, especially, analogies or stories. Make your speech interesting, both visually and verbally. The best way to reach your audience with your message is to deliver it in an entertaining way — without, of course, making a fool of yourself or getting side-tracked.

10. Be aware of your timing. Either place your watch on the lectern — out of sight — or ensure beforehand that there is a wall clock within easy viewing. However, don't ever make it obvious that you are clock-watching, you don't want your audience to think that you would rather not be there. Here's what is known as "The Speaker's Prayer", which you might find useful — I know I sometimes do: "Lord, fill my mouth with all good stuff and nudge me when I've said enough."

What if I'm nervous?

Unfortunately, there is no magic formula for overcoming nerves. Every speaker has suffered with nerves at one time or another, and many regular speakers still admit to feeling nervous prior to starting a speech — including myself sometimes. At the end of the day, the only way to overcome nervousness or fear is by doing the thing you fear to do. However, having said that, let me now give you one or two guidelines which you might find helpful.

First off, if you are nervous, then initially don't make eye contact with members of the audience. It might only take someone with a critical expression on their face to throw you completely off balance. Instead, start off by looking just over the heads of as many people as possible. Then, as you get into your speech and your confidence grows, you can begin making eye contact.

Secondly, talking about something that you know about, something that you have a real passion for, is one of the best solutions there is for overcoming nerves. So, choose your subject well.

To finish, here is another verse to encourage and inspire you. Unfortunately, the author's name is unknown to me, but the verse is titled "Believe In Yourself".

> *Believe in yourself! You're divinely designed,*
> *And perfectly made for the work of mankind.*
> *This truth you must cling to through danger and pain,*
> *The heights man has reached you can also attain.*
>
> *Believe to the very last hour, for it's true,*
> *That whatever you will, you've been gifted to do.*
> *Believe in yourself and step out unafraid,*
> *By misgivings and doubt be not easily swayed.*
>
> *You've the right to succeed, the precision of skill*
> *Which betokens the great, you can earn if you will!*
> *The wisdom of ages is yours if you'll read,*
> *But you've got to believe in yourself to succeed.*

And finally, you might take further inspiration and encouragement from the following words of advice from the Bible, written by King Solomon: "Commit to the Lord whatever you do, and your plans will succeed." (Proverbs 16:3) I wish you well, and, in signing off, let me say: good luck, God bless and goodbye for now.

Yours cordially,

Uncle Bob

CHAPTER SIX

Self-Motivation

Dear Go-getter,

EVERYONE, INCLUDING MYSELF, suffers from apathy, lethargy and "I can't switch myself on" syndrome from time to time. It is virtually impossible to stay motivated, to remain on a high, 24 hours a day, 7 days a week, 52 weeks a year. Now, of course, some people are more motivated than others — and I like to think of myself as being in that category — but the fact is that everyone, and I do mean everyone, suffers from a dose of the dumps every once in a while. We all have the same feelings and emotions, and we all think and behave in a very similar manner.

To prove my point about our all being alike, try this light-hearted exercise. Answer the following questions as quickly as you can and without changing your mind:

1. Pick a number between 1 and 10 and stick with it.

2. Multiply that number by 9. (This will test your multiplication skills!)

3. Next, subtract 5 from your answer.

4. Is the number you now have a single-digit number (e.g. 1, 2 or 3) or a double-digit number (e.g. 11, 22 or 33)? If it is a single-

digit number, stick with it and move on to step 5 below. On the other hand, if your answer is a double-digit number, add the two digits together. (For example, if your answer was 14, add the 1 and the 4 together to get 5.) Now, is your answer a single- or double-digit number? Repeat this process of adding the two digits together until you arrive at a single-digit number.

5. Next, using the number you now have, find the corresponding letter of the alphabet, where A=1, B=2, C=3 and so on.

6. Now, think of a country beginning with that letter.

7. Then, take the second letter of that country, and think of an animal beginning with that letter.

8. Finally, think of the colour of that animal.

The above exercise works on the principle that human minds think alike (9 times out of 10, anyway). Hopefully, your answer will agree with mine, which can be found at the foot of Page 59. (If it doesn't, well, I'm sure it was close enough, otherwise you could always try it again.)

The point behind this little exercise is not simply to entertain you, but to show you that we all think alike, each and every one of us. We all have the same needs, wants and desires, and we all have the same feelings. Understand, then, that feeling down every once in a while is, if you are human, inevitable. As I said in a previous letter, life is full of peaks and troughs, of mountain-top and valley-floor experiences. And the key to having more peaks than troughs in life is knowing how to pull yourself up by the bootstraps and switch yourself on again. How, then, you might ask, is a person able to do this, to switch himself or herself on again? In this letter, I shall endeavour to give you a few pointers which will, hopefully, help you to answer that question.

Let me start by relating a true story to you about my own self-motivation. When I was a late-teenager, I started up my first business. I had just passed my driving test, and now I had a new goal: I wanted to have my very my own "set of wheels", so that I could be independent and, more importantly, mobile.

However, there was just one obstacle: I didn't have the money, or the available means of obtaining sufficient quantities of it, to buy a car. (I wasn't able to lean on my parents.) At the time, I was studying at college and holding down a full-time job which, as I remember, paid just $50 a week. So, there was no way I could afford to buy a car, let alone pay for the insurance, maintenance and running costs involved in keeping one on the road.

Still, my goal was a passionate one, and the desire to have my own set of wheels caused me to think up all sorts of ideas and possible ways of achieving my objective. Eventually, I came up with a plan of action, and, after some "creative" paperwork, I was able to purchase a small second-hand van on credit, without actually putting down a deposit. As I recall, the finance payments were around $150 per month over 36 months, which at the time represented three out of every four of my weekly pay-packets.

My intention was to earn enough extra money to be able to pay for my vehicle. To do this, my plan was to sell groceries door to door by setting up an evening delivery round on a housing estate for the elderly. The plan worked. I was friendly with a local shopkeeper and I gave all the orders to him. In return, he agreed to package and price all the goods for me so that all I had to do was collect the goods from his shop and deliver them back to the customer's door, making 20 per cent commission for my efforts.

This proved to be a win-win-win situation. The shopkeeper was happy, because he sold more of his goods. My customers were mostly older people, some of them quite frail, so they were happy, too, because my service meant that they didn't have to rely so much on others or carry heavy shopping themselves. They also received excellent-quality goods, value for money, and service with a smile — even if I do say so myself. And then, of course, I was happy. In fact, the business did so well that I was able to pay off the finance on the vehicle in just over a year, instead of three years, as originally planned.

Now, of course, it wasn't all a bed of roses. In the beginning, there was a lot of footwork, door-knocking and rejection involved. I can remember, after the first week, feeling dejected and miserable at the constant rejections, and the cloud of impending doom hanging over my head as the first finance payment loomed on my calendar. I remember wanting so much to pack it all in, to take the van back to the dealers and say, "I'm sorry, I made a mistake, please can you cancel the credit agreement and take the keys back?"

Of course, that wasn't possible, and if I failed, the finance company would have taken legal action to recover the debt. I had no choice but to persist with my endeavours. Night after night I trudged the streets, knocking on doors and trying to persuade the inhabitants to give me a trial run and place an order. In fact, it was here, during this very experience, that I first learnt the all-important principle (which I have mentioned before) that persistence always conquers resistance, eventually.

In reading the above account, you will see that the main ingredient that motivated me to succeed was necessity. Once I had made an irrevocable commitment to the finance company, there was no going back or giving up. In summary, then, it was the necessity to produce results, coupled with the fear of failure, that motivated me to succeed. At the end of the day, to simply give up wasn't an option that was open to me — otherwise, I would probably have taken it.

As I mentioned earlier, the key to having more peaks than troughs in life is knowing how to pull yourself up by the bootstraps and switch yourself on again. Following on from this, I thought it would be useful to share some ideas with you, and show you how to actually do this. I have, therefore, compiled the following list, to inspire and motivate you into action.

A dozen different ways to help motivate yourself

1. *Set a goal, then burn your bridges by making an irrevocable commitment to achieve that goal*

    Here is another example of the self-motivation technique I have just been discussing, the "do or die" formula (to "burn your

---

In the quiz, were you thinking of a grey elephant in Denmark?

bridges" is to make something impossible to return to — another version of this saying, with the same meaning, is to "burn your boats"):

> In ancient times, invaders would sail to foreign shores, their goal to conquer, plunder and pillage. They would decide upon a destination, prepare themselves for battle and then set sail. As soon as they landed on the alien shore, they would make their commitment irrevocable by setting their boats on fire and destroying them. (Hence the expression, "to burn your boats".) By doing so, they made the ultimate decision. Now, there would be no going back or staying put. From there on in, it was do or die, victory or defeat.

How's that for self-motivation?

I am reminded here of a quote by Sir Winston Churchill, which still remains good advice today. In a speech accredited as one of the longest public addresses in history to say only seven words, Churchill, in his deep voice and slow manner, told his audience, "Never give in ... Never ... Never ... Never ... Never!" (It was because of Churchill's stubborn tenacity that he was nicknamed the "British bulldog". It was also this attribute that earned him much success.)

So, then, to motivate yourself into action, set yourself a goal, burn your bridges (or boats), make an irrevocable commitment to achieve your goal and never give in ... Never!

2. *Consider things over time and not on the spur of the moment*
   When you're feeling down, instead of focusing on the present, focus on the past and take an overall view of your performance. Consider your prior achievements and successes over a period of, say, six months and you'll see that, all in all, you are a success, not a failure.

In the past, you have been successful, haven't you? That much is fact. Now let me ask you this question: Do you think you will ever succeed again in the future? Of course you will. There is no doubt in your mind about that, is there? So, why not decide to use this insight to influence and inspire you back into action right now?

Understand that being "down in the dumps", so to speak, is only ever temporary: it is like the passing of a shadow. But also consider this: "If there were no shadows, there would be no sunshine." Often, you only need to realise this and it will be enough to move you out of the shadows and back into the light. And it doesn't matter how thick or dark your clouds are, because, as some other wise person once said, "Even through the thickest, darkest clouds the sun is still shining brightly." Consider things over time, not on the spur of the moment, and you will climb up through the clouds, you'll move out of the shadows and back into the sunshine again.

3. *Motivate yourself by motivating others*

"When you bend to help lift another to their feet, you can't help but lift yourself at the same time." Think about it. When you motivate others, it has an echo effect, inasmuch as what you send out comes back to you — it's the boomerang principle again. Some wise and humorous person once put it this way: "Good deeds, like chickens, always come home to roost." That's a lovely way of putting it, and one that is very pertinent to the point I am trying to make here. Go out of your way to motivate and encourage others and you will end up motivating and encouraging yourself in the process.

So, when you are feeling down, instead of wallowing in your sorrow, look around you and see if you can offer a helping hand to another in need. Remember, it is in giving that we receive — which leads us nicely on to the next technique.

4. *Talk with a positive person*

This, too, has a knock-on effect. A positive person is an enthusiastic person, and enthusiasm is highly contagious. So, seek them out for all you are worth, feed off them and become stimulated back into action. Staying with the theme of talking, you should also talk positively to yourself, which is the next technique.

5. *Use positive self-talk or affirmations*

Remember, the human mind is like a magnet: it always attracts that which dominates our thinking. So, to motivate yourself into action, use positive self-talk or affirmations, and condition your mind to attract whatever it is you think about. (My next letter will be focused entirely on this subject.)

6. *Don't mope around, just do it*

Abraham Lincoln once said, "Things may come to those who wait, but only the things left by those who hustle." And that is exactly what you must do to switch yourself on again: hustle, and jump into action. In other words, don't mope around, just do it. Let me demonstrate the point with the following tale:

> Two neighbours, Donald and Mickey, were fishing in the mountain lakes, when they spotted a big grizzly bear foraging for food nearby. No sooner had they seen it than the grizzly also seemed to notice them, and with a mean look on its face the bear began to approach slowly. "Look at that bear," said Donald. "I wonder if it means to eat us?" Mickey, who was something of a know-it-all, replied, "Well, bears are carnivorous, and they have been known to attack the odd fisherman or two, and also people who startle them. They can run at speeds of up to 30 miles an hour over short distances, so there's no way we can outrun it. The only thing in our favour right now is that bears have very poor eyesight. So, our best line of defence is to stay perfectly still and quiet and then, hopefully, he will pass us by."
>
> With that, Donald, who was highly motivated not to be eaten alive, opened his back-pack, took out his running shoes and began putting them on. "What are you doing that for?" said Mickey. "I have told you there is no way you can outrun a bear." Unperturbed, Donald

continued doing up his runners. Then, as he turned to make his escape, he answered, "The way I see it, Mickey, I don't have to outrun the bear. All I have to do is outrun you!"

The moral of this little tale is: don't mope about waiting for things to get better by themselves; instead, take action and do something about it now. Just do it!

7. *Listen to motivational material*

I always find that listening to motivational music gives me a big lift, and I frequently find myself strumming along with my fingers, whistling, humming, singing or tapping my feet to a tune that I have listened to several hours before. In fact, I have even compiled a tape of my own favourite songs from various artists. Why not do the same? Similarly, listening to a motivational speaker can be very uplifting. It might interest you to know that I have several hundred hours' worth of audio programmes in my own collection, and there is always a cassette in my Walkman.

8. *Read a good book*

Much of my own inspiration and motivation comes from reading non-fiction material — self-help books, business books, Christian books, autobiographies and so on. I own several hundred of these, and I always have a book on the go. In the following verse, the poet John Wilson captures my own sentiments about reading:

> *O for a book and a shady nook,*
> *Either in the door or out;*
> *With green leaves whispering overhead,*
> *Or the street cries all about,*
> *Where I may read all at my ease,*
> *Both of the new and old;*
> *For a jolly good book whereon to look,*
> *Is better to me than gold.*

9. *Clap hands*

When you are feeling lethargic or sluggish, and you need that instant boost to motivate and turn yourself on, try clapping your hands together — slowly and deliberately at first, and then gradually, over the next 20 seconds or so, increasing in speed until you literally cannot clap any faster. This action creates a similar sensation to that of listening to up-beat music: it increases your own physical tempo, which in turn flips your attitude switch to the "on" position.

10. *Dress up and go up*

Essentially, what I'm talking about here is creating that all-important feel-good factor. If you dress up, look smart, polish your shoes, get a haircut, have a manicure, and so on, you will look good and feel good about yourself.

As an example, I read recently that, in the United States, many poor-performance schools have reported a massive improvement in attitude after they introduced compulsory wearing of uniforms. Beforehand, students were allowed to wear whatever they liked — within reason, of course. Things like jeans, leather jackets with chains and studs, cowboy boots and football shirts were the norm, and the overall attitude and motivation of the pupils reflected this "wear what you like" dress policy. However, when uniforms were introduced (along with financial assistance when there was a proven need), the attitude and motivation of the pupils changed dramatically. It was simply a case of "dress up and go up". Try it.

11. *Take a walk-and-talk session*

This is one of the things I often do when I'm feeling down or need inspiration. Take some time out alone, go off for a long walk and talk with your Creator. Whatever it is that's bothering you, get it off your chest, just let go and talk openly. You'll feel so much better afterwards. Then, in faith, ask God for fresh inspiration and direction, ask Him to show you the way forward and to motivate you back into action.

A few years ago, I was given a short verse written by the late Helen Steiner Rice. In reading it, I am always reminded that if we don't ask, we won't get. The rhyme is so simple, and yet at the same time so profound. Here it is:

> *Games can't be won unless they are played,*
> *And prayers can't be answered unless they are prayed.*

12. *Take a break and treat yourself*

No doubt, you will have heard the expression, "All work and no play makes Jack a dull boy." Sometimes, the best way to revitalise and motivate yourself is with a tonic. Whether it is a break from the regular routine, a new outfit or a new toy, the "treat yourself" routine is a good way to refresh, restore and invigorate yourself.

Sometimes, the problem lies in motivating yourself to actually start work. When this is the case, here's a good idea: set yourself an immediate-term goal and then reward yourself when you achieve it. For example, you might say to yourself, "My target is to make ten calls today. When I achieve my target, I'll buy myself that portable CD player that I've had my eye on." In other words, create an incentive for yourself. Treat yourself.

The act of rewarding worthy performance is also a good management technique for motivating others to perform whatever task you may ask of them. It is a well-known fact that rewarding good performance always encourages repeat performance. Think about it: if a child draws you a picture and you reward the child by showering praise on him or her for the wonderful masterpiece they have created, what happens? That's right, the child is encouraged, and goes off to draw you another one — and another, and another.

This same technique of rewarding good performance to motivate and encourage repeat performance is also used by animal trainers. For instance, I'm sure you will have seen the likes of a dolphin show at some time or another. When a dolphin performs a trick, the trainer throws it a tidbit, both as a reward and to encourage repeat performance.

To recap, then: take a break and treat yourself, or create an incentive to reward your improved performance and motivate yourself into action.

So, there you have it. A dozen different ways to help motivate yourself. Let me finish off with another management principle pertaining to motivation. Managers — and everyone is a manager of one sort or another — should manage using motivation and not manipulation. Let me elaborate, using the following story, from the Second World War, as an example:

> Before he became the 34th President of the United States, General Dwight D. Eisenhower was one of the most successful military commanders in history. The story goes that in order to explain and illustrate to his officers the important leadership skill of motivating and not manipulating the troops, General Eisenhower would place a piece of string on the floor. He would then demonstrate that by going behind the string and pushing it, he got nowhere — the string just wanted to rebel and go its own way. However, on the other hand, when he took the lead and pulled the string, it would follow him obediently in whichever direction he chose to go.

The lesson in motivation is clear: we should pull, not push. Pushing others, or yourself, too hard, or forcing yourself to do something that you don't really want to do, means that any movement will only ever be made reluctantly — which, of course, causes friction and stress. On the other hand, if you pull the right strings (motivate, not manipulate), you will motivate yourself into action, and that response will come without friction. So, don't push — pull.

Well, it's now time for me to push off (excuse the pun), so until next time, keep your chin up, and remember, "Behind every shadow there's always a light shining."

Yours cordially,

Uncle Bob

CHAPTER SEVEN

The Powerful Force of Positive Thinking

Dear Go-getter,

WHAT I SHALL attempt to do in this letter is, first of all, explain the "powerful force of positive thinking", and then go on to demonstrate how you can utilise this power source to bring about the desires of your own heart.

Let me start by recommending a book for you to read (that is, if you haven't already done so). This famous book, which I have mentioned before, was originally published back in 1953 and was written by the late Dr Norman Vincent Peale. When I first read it, many years ago, it made a lasting impression on me and has had a very profound effect on my own life. I am obviously not alone in my praise for Dr Peale's book, as it has become one of the world's all-time best-selling classics, having sold well over 15 million copies. The book is titled *The Power of Positive Thinking*, and in it Dr Peale gives his formula for success using the power of prayer and positive thinking. Basically, the formula has three steps to it, being:

1. Prayerise
2. Picturise
3. Actualise.

Obviously, from a religious point of view, everyone is free to believe whatever they choose, but I think you should know where I stand on this issue: as a committed Christian, I agree 100 per cent with Dr Peale's philosophy.

Furthermore, the way I see it is this: when God created the world, he didn't create it through physical labour — at least, not in the sense that we would define physical labour. Instead, the Bible tells us that God gave a command and it was so. The Bible also tells us that God made man in His own image, and this, then, implies that we share many of God's characteristics. One thing is for certain: we all have the supernatural ability to attract that which we think about.

No one has ever fully understood how this process actually works, nor will we ever fully understand it — not in this lifetime, anyway. However, there is no doubt that it does work. Indeed, practically everyone has experienced proof of it working in their own lives in some form or another. Take, for example, the number of times you have been thinking about a particular person, then the phone rings and that very person is on the other end of the line. Some people call this a coincidence, others call it a "God-incidence". Just because we don't fully understand how our thoughts produce the corresponding results doesn't mean that it doesn't happen.

It's like eating an apple: when we eat an apple, we know that the apple will provide us with some of the nourishment we need. Our bodies, which are the most sophisticated and advanced laboratories in the world, will produce enough chemical enzymes to break the apple down into various vitamins, sugars, fats, proteins, minerals and so on. Some parts of the apple might be used in strengthening a fingernail, some for creating saliva or whatever else the body needs. Just how it works no one actually knows, but the fact that it does work is irrefutable. Scientists and biologists can prove that much.

We also know that the heart pumps blood around the body to provide oxygen, nutrients, white blood cells to fight bacteria, and so on: that much, again, can be proved. But what we can't prove and don't know is what makes it all work. What makes the heart work — the brain? Yes, but what makes the brain work?

So, you see, no one on the face of the earth fully understands the gift of life, nor does anyone fully understand how the workings of our mind can bring about powerful manifestations — no one, that is, except God.

The fact is that we don't really need to fully understand how it works to know that it does work. This is what is known as having faith. Going back to the apple again, we don't need to fully understand what actually happens to the apple to know that it feeds us. Likewise, with positive thinking, we don't need to fully understand the exact process of what happens to know that it does, in fact, happen. The whole idea of faith as taught in the Bible is that believing is seeing, not the other way around. Jesus himself said, "If you believe you will receive whatever you ask for in prayer." (Matthew 21:22) Now, that's positive: believing is seeing.

Remaining on the same theme, I once read the following note, in which the anonymous author encourages us to get into action, to use our heads or, to paraphrase the message, to think positively:

When God created us He gave us two ends,
One to sit on and one to think with.
Success depends upon which end we use most,
Heads we win and tails we lose!

At the end of the day, each and every one of us has the ability to produce fantastic and wonderful results by utilising our ability to think. Now, that is not to say that with positive thinking we can create the impossible. For example, a 40-year-old man weighing 90 kilograms who hasn't done any form of exercise in his entire adult life will never become Mr Universe, no matter how much positive thinking he gives to the idea. However, that same man, with positive thinking and determined action, although he may not produce the impossible, can still produce fantastic and wonderful results. The outcome of an event, be it positive or negative, is first of all determined in the mind.

The mind of man has often been the subject of debate, and yet the more that scientists and psychologists come to understand about the mind and human brain, the more unfathomable it becomes. For example, in a recent British television programme, titled "The Richard Dimbleby Lecture", the Oxford University biologist Professor Richard Hawkins said, discussing the enormous potential of a man's mind, "If you unravelled a man's brain cells and placed them end to end, there would be enough to go around the world 25 times." Now, that's what I call astronomical!

A further example can be found in the runaway best-selling book *Psycho-Cybernetics*, where the author, Maxwell Maltz, quotes the British neurophysicist W. Grey Walter as having once said the following:

> At least ten billion electronic cells would be needed to build a facsimile of a man's brain. These cells would occupy about a million and a half cubic feet, and several additional millions of cubic feet would be needed for the 'nerves' or wiring. The power to operate it would be around a billion watts.

Yes indeed, our human brain, our mind, is so powerful that we can't even come close to comprehending what we are capable of achieving (when we put our minds to it, that is).

However, although we will never fully comprehend the capacity of the mind, or how it actually works, it is now widely accepted that we are able to condition our mind to attract that which we think about, to create the outcome of an event, be it positive or negative. The best way I can put it into words is to paraphrase an old saying: "Ours is not to question why, ours is to accept that it works and give it a try." And that is what I am suggesting you do here: accept that it does work and try it for yourself. The results might not be instantaneous, but they will come, if you just stick with it.

Mind the Garden of Your Mind

It has been said that our minds resemble a garden, and, like all gardens, if they are not cultivated and looked after constantly, weeds and unwanted plants will soon take root, grow, and multiply in abundance. It is the same with the human mind, which is itself a fertile and productive garden. We must feed our mind with positive thoughts if we wish to produce and harvest positive results. Again, we are told in the Bible, "A man reaps what he sows." (Galatians 6:7) Allowing our mind to think negative thoughts is like ignoring our garden and allowing the weeds to set in and spread like wildfire. In other words, if we do not think positive, then our mind cannot help but become overrun with the weeds of negativity. So, we must be very careful as to what thoughts we will allow into our mind. As soon as a negative thought surfaces, you should expel it — forcefully, if need be.

How do you do this? Well, although we can't stop negative thoughts occurring, we can decide whether to run with the thought or whether to dismiss it from our mind. William James, the famous American philosopher and psychologist, once said, "The greatest discovery of my generation is that human beings can alter their lives by altering their attitudes of mind." And we all have the power to do this. We can only think of one thing at any given time, and the exciting thing is that we can control our thoughts. We can decide what it is that we think about.

Let me give you an example. I want you to stop reading for a second or two and think about an ice-cream cone; picture it in your mind. Now, dismiss that thought and, instead, think about a child riding a bicycle down a hill. Okay, that was easy enough, wasn't it? You were able to control your thoughts, you were able to dismiss one and replace it with another of your own choice. You should do the very same thing whenever a negative thought pays you a visit.

Unfortunately, in everyday life, we are surrounded by many negative influences. Every day, we are bombarded with pessimism from work colleagues, customers, neighbours and so on. Every day, we listen to the news or read a newspaper and are subjected to disasters and to the daily doom and gloom of our society. Although we can't ignore these negative influences or hide ourselves away from them, we can control how we will react to such influences.

For example, if someone started throwing raw sewage at you, what would you do? Would you simply stand there and take it, or would you do everything within your power to stop them?

It is exactly the same when the media or other people are poisoning your mind with negativity. You can decide whether to stand there and take it or whether to do something positive about it. Now, I am not suggesting you always simply turn a deaf ear to what is going on around you, or ignore another person's cry for help. (In any event, helping another person is generally a positive response.) What I am saying is that you have the capacity to decide how you will react to a negative situation: you can decide to allow the attack of negative thoughts to get to you, or you can decide to dismiss them from your mind and change your thinking and subsequent actions to a more positive mode.

As another example, if you are watching violence, disaster, obscenity or the like on television, you can choose to go along with these negative influences, or you can choose to do something positive and either switch over to another channel or turn off. Some people say that their thinking is not influenced by watching television, but they're wrong. It's just that the influence is so subtle that it is not so easily recognisable. After all, there are thousands of companies that spend millions of dollars on television advertising every day to do just that: influence the viewing public. They wouldn't continue to spend all that money on advertising if it didn't work.

So, then, how do you go about actually conditioning your mind to attract success? Well, conditioning the mind works very much on the same principle as programming a computer. Maybe you are familiar with the term "GIGO" (pronounced "gee-go"), taken from the computer-programming industry. It is an acronym of the words "Garbage In, Garbage Out", meaning that the performance of a computer (its output) is only determined by what was put into the computer in the first place. It is the same with the human mind: garbage in, garbage out. Just as a computer has a rubbish bin or a delete button, so we have a delete button of our own, and the capacity to remove an unwanted thought or message.

For example, if you're not feeling so good, don't say to yourself or others, "I feel dreadful." If you say that, you are actually reinforcing the thought and programming your mind to, indeed, feel dreadful. Instead, when you catch yourself in this negative mode of thinking, stop yourself — press your delete button to get rid of the negative affirmation and then reprogram the message you are sending to yourself, by saying, "I want to feel well again." In other words, replace the negative thought by rephrasing or paraphrasing it in a more positive way. What you are really doing is giving your mind a command; you're saying to the computer of your mind, "I want to feel well again." And just as a computer is programmed to obey commands, so too is your own mind.

Still in the computer industry, here is another acronym, WYSIWYG (pronounced "wiz-ee-wig"), meaning, "What You See Is What You Get." And that really is the key to positive thinking: what you see (or what you think about) is what you get.

So, you see, it is very important that we fill our minds with positive thoughts. Whenever you catch yourself thinking negatively — and we all do from time to time — stop yourself. Take control of the thought — by shaking your head, if you have to. Then, change your thinking: replace the negative thought with a positive one. Finally, program or condition your mind to remain positive by repeating positive affirmations to yourself. Basically, what I'm saying is: be an optimist, think positive, expect results and have the faith to believe that, whatever it is, it can and will happen. Again, Jesus told us, "According to your faith will it be done to you." (Matthew 9:29) In the Bible, the apostle Paul also gives us some excellent advice about positive thinking: "Whatever is true, whatever is noble, whatever is right, whatever is pure, whatever is lovely, whatever is admirable — if anything is excellent or praiseworthy — think about such things." (Philippians 4:8) You can't get much more positive than that.

Decorating the wall of my study I have a verse which was written by someone who, although anonymous, most definitely understood the powerful force of positive thinking. The verse is titled "The Man Who Thinks He Can". I have copied it down for you on the next page.

If you think you are beaten, you are,
If you think you dare not, you don't.
If you like to win, but think you can't,
It is almost certain you won't.

If you think you'll lose, you're lost,
For out in the world we find,
Success begins with a fellow's will,
It's all in the state of mind.

If you think you're outclassed, you are,
You've got to think high to rise,
You've got to be sure of yourself before
You can ever win a prize.

Life's battles don't always go
To the stronger or faster man,
But sooner or later, the man who wins,
Is the man who thinks he can!

And that's just it. If you think you can, you can, and if you think you can't, you can't: it is all down to the way we think. Ralph Waldo Emerson (1803–1882) said, "A man is what he thinks about all day long." What Emerson was saying is that when you have a passion for something — something that you are constantly working towards, something that you continually think about — whatever it is will come to pass, be it positive or negative. If you think success, you will ultimately succeed. If you think failure, you will ultimately fail.

When all is said and done, what it all boils down to is that the mind of man is an extraordinary source of power. Think about it: everything created by man begins with a thought. Just look around you right now as you read these words. Every single thing that you set your eyes on that is man-made began as a thought in the mind of somebody, even down to the chair you are sitting on and these papers you are holding in your hand. Everything that is created by man originates from thought. Awesome, isn't it?

So, you see, our minds, our thoughts, are so very, very powerful. We must be careful, therefore, to concentrate on the things we want, not on the things we don't want, because whatever it is that dominates our thinking comes into being. Our mind works like a magnet to attract that which we think about, be it positive or negative. I understand that when a piece of steel is magnetised, it is capable of lifting about 12 times its own weight. But, of course, when it is demagnetised, it can't even pick up a feather. It is the same with us: if we are positive, switched on, magnetised, then we can accomplish great feats; but if we are negative, demagnetised, then we will accomplish nothing.

There is an old Chinese proverb which says, "If you give a man a fish you feed him for a day, but if you teach him how to fish you feed him for a lifetime." What I would like to do now is give you a fishing lesson and show you how to condition your mind for success. First, a little preparation, in the form of a true story about how I first discovered the power of positive thinking, as a schoolboy. Incidentally, whenever I have shared this story with an audience, I am amazed at how many people are able to relate to it because they have had a similar experience.

The story begins when I was 12 years old. During the summer holidays, my brothers and I went to stay with my grandmother, by the coast. Being boys and by the sea, one of our favourite pastimes was fishing, but, not being able to afford the luxury of having fishing rods, we had to improvise. When it was low tide, we would go down to the water's edge and drive two large stakes, each nearly two metres high, into the sand, putting rocks around the base to secure them. We would place the posts about six metres apart and leave about one metre of each post protruding out of the sand.

Next, we would tie fishing line, with hooks and bait, between the posts, and then stand back and wait for the tide to turn. After half an hour or so, our "night-line", as we used to call it, would be submerged, which meant it was safe for us to leave it alone. (There were no bathers where we used to do this.) For the next 12 hours and 25 minutes, until the next low tide, our night-line would be under several feet of water — hopefully, tempting any passing fish to stop for a nibble. Well, as luck would have it, 12½ hours later, when it was low tide again and time for us to check our lines, it always seemed to be around 4 or 5 o'clock — in the morning! This meant that if we were to salvage our catch from the local seagulls, we would have to get up really early. This is where my discovery comes into the story.

The problem was that we didn't have an alarm clock with us, and so I was once again forced to improvise. (As I'm sure you are aware, schoolboys of that age very rarely have a use for alarm clocks, and especially not during school holidays.) At night, as I lay in bed, I would picture the hands of a clock pointing to 4 o'clock. With this picture held firmly in my mind's eye, I would then repeat, over and over, until I dropped off to sleep, "I *must* wake up at 4 o'clock, I *will* wake up at 4 o'clock." The next morning, when I opened my eyes and looked at my watch, I was always within a minute or two of my designated time.

I had fallen upon a secret — the secret of attracting that which we think about. Over the years, I began, and continue, to use this technique, to better and better effect. At the time, it seemed incredible to me that simply by picturing a scene in my mind and then repeating positive affirmations over and over, with real conviction, I was able to attract or bring about what I was thinking about.

For a long time, I thought that my secret technique would seem not so much incredible as downright silly to other people, so I kept it to myself for fear of being ridiculed. Then, some years later, whilst reading books written by successful people, especially Dr Peale's book, I discovered that my secret was not really my secret at all. I can remember feeling shocked to read that other people were using my technique to condition their minds for success; only it seemed that some were achieving far better results than I was. It was then that I discovered the reason for this: those individuals were incorporating another element into the technique that, up until then, I had not been including myself — namely, that of prayer.

I have since made my own adaptation of Dr Peale's formula for success. Mine goes like this: prayerise; visualise; verbalise; materialise. Let us briefly look at how the four-step formula works in practice:

1. First of all, *prayerise* — lift your requests in faith to God.

2. Then, condition your mind for success and *visualise* whatever it is as already having happened (that is, visualise it in the past tense). This is very important, because if you visualise something as if it is going to happen — in the future tense — then it always will remain just that: in the future.

3. Next, to strengthen your faith and shake off any doubts or negative thoughts that may be trying to get a foothold, you need to *verbalise* — that is, repeat positive affirmations to yourself, and say them with strength and conviction. Again, make sure you use only positive words. For example, don't say, "I won't fail the exam." Instead, say, "I will pass the exam."

4. Finally, stick with the programme, have faith and don't give up, because sooner or later your desire will *materialise*. Remember, persistence always conquers resistance, eventually.

Oliver Wendell Holmes wrote, "Man's mind, once stretched by a new idea, never regains its original dimensions." I hope that you will stretch your mind, I hope that you will think big and, using the above information, strive to achieve great things. One of the reasons why a lot of people aren't more successful than they are is simply that they don't think big enough.

This reminds me of the story of the frog at the bottom of the well. When the frog looked up, he thought the sky was only as big as the top of the well, so he stayed where he was until he died. (Remember WYSIWYG? What You See Is What You Get.) The frog's thinking was too small. Had he climbed to the top of the well, the frog would have seen just how much more of the world there actually is. The same applies with our own thinking: if you think small, you will only ever see small results; but if you stretch yourself, think big and keep climbing, you will start to see big results.

I will leave you with the words of Napoleon Hill, author of another classic and best-selling book, titled *Think and Grow Rich*: "Whatever the mind of man can conceive and believe it will achieve." Now, that should certainly give you something to think about.

Yours positively,

Uncle Bob

CHAPTER EIGHT

How to Conquer Fear

Dear Go-getter,

NOW AND AGAIN we all need to be reminded of certain things, so I have decided to dedicate my next few letters to doing just that: reminding you of certain issues that actually stand in the way of success. In this letter I shall be looking at fear.

Everybody experiences some kind of fear, practically every day of their lives. Now, that is a bold statement, but when you consider that fear has variable strengths, and many disguises, you will see that it is true. For instance, fear can come in the form of apprehension, worry, anxiety, panic, alarm, doubt, uncertainty, horror, awe and fright, and many other guises. Then there is fear for one's safety or welfare, fear of the unknown, fear of making the wrong decision, fear of failure, fear of change, fear of something new — the list is endless.

Whenever we feel threatened, whenever we are faced with a situation that causes uncertainty, apprehension or fear, we react in one of two ways: either we stand and fight or we turn and flee. This reaction has been termed the "fight or flight" response. The *fight* response is, obviously, to dig your heels in and refuse to be intimidated by the fear, even though you may feel it strongly. It is to pluck up the necessary courage, to pull yourself up by the bootstraps, to take action, to fight the fear and persevere. This is the response of a person with a winning attitude and, of course, it is the response needed to succeed.

On the other hand, the *flight* response is to run away or hide away from the problem, hoping that it will go away by itself. It is to allow the fear to have the upper hand, to avoid taking action, to delay or put off making a decision about what course of action to take. Let me put it like this: failure says, "Run, run, run away and live to confront your fears another day." Success says, "Stand, stand, stand today and overcome your fears straight away."

The fact is that fear is one of the biggest obstacles to success, because fear is the biggest cause of indecision. (I shall cover this topic in more depth in my next letter.) The famous British mathematician, philosopher and writer Bertrand Russell once said, "Fear is the main source of superstition, and one of the main sources of cruelty. To conquer fear is the beginning of wisdom." Think about it: some people have so succumbed to superstition and the fear of making the wrong decision that their lives are now completely governed by horoscopes, clairvoyants, biorhythms and so on.

This kind of fear, really, is the opposite of faith. It is the kind of fear that kills a person's potential and causes insecurity and failure. It is the fear based on superstition and dread, and unless you kill this particular fear, unless you avoid such practices and leave them well alone, they could, in the end, cause you a great deal of harm. I very much like what the author David Watson says on this subject: "Fear is the opposite of faith ... it is faith in what you do not want to happen." Understand this: it is impossible to have faith and fear at the same time. Think about it.

The Secret of Conquering Fear

The truth of the matter is that we all know the secret of how to overcome fear. Let's clear away a few cobwebs and go back in time for a moment or two, and have a look at how you have dealt with some of your own fears in the past.

1. Remember your (or your child's) first day at school. Can you recall the fear, the panic of being left alone and abandoned, the

tears, the yelling? What did you do to overcome those feelings? Stop reading, and think about it for a moment.

2. Think back to the time you asked that special girl or boy for a date. Probably, you were shy, nervous, maybe stuttering a little and fumbling over your words. How did you subdue that fear of being rejected, enough to go ahead and ask the person out? What did you do?

3. Can you recollect the day of your driving test, when you were so nervous that your knees wouldn't stop shaking? How did you cope? What did you have to do in order to take the exam?

4. How about your first job interview, your first day at work, or having to make that sales call? How did you manage to defeat those attacks of cold feet and apprehension?

5. Or what about the day of your wedding, or the first time you ever spoke publicly to an audience? Were you nervous? Did you keep swallowing? Was your voice trembling with fear and apprehension? How on earth did you manage to get through that experience? What did you have to do?

6. Do you recall those sleepless nights after hearing the rumour that redundancies were in the air at work, or the time when you were deliberating over that very expensive purchase? Again, how did you deal with your fear and get through those times?

7. Finally, if you are a parent, try to remember how you felt on the day your first child was born. When you realised that the labour had started, was it excited anticipation or panic, or maybe a mixture of both, that caused those butterflies to flutter in your stomach? Once again, how did you overcome your fear?

I am confident that everybody can relate to at least one of the above examples, but one thing I am sure of is that everyone — and I do mean everyone — knows the secret of how to conquer fear. The problem is, most people either don't know that they know the secret, or forget that they know it. For the sake of clarity, let me give it to you again now. But not in my words — rather, let me quote to you the words of Ralph Waldo Emerson, who wrote, "Do the thing you fear to do and the death of fear is certain."

And that's it, that's the simple truth. If you go back to the seven illustrations above, you will see that, in every example you were able to relate to, the way you overcame your fear was simply to get on and do the thing you feared to do. Here is a short verse that I wrote as a reminder to myself to do the very same thing.

Do the Thing You Fear to Do

Don't let fear get a hold on you,
Instead, do the thing you fear to do.
If you're lost and not sure which path to take,
Listen to your heart, the truth it won't fake.

But you won't find the courage by waiting around,
So get down off the fence and move onto solid ground.
Then, when you've overcome the fear,
*   you'll look back and see,*
That it wasn't as bad as you thought it would be.

So don't let fear get a hold on you,
Instead, do the thing you fear to do,
And next time fear raises its ugly head,
Jump straight into action and kill the fear, dead!

Fear is an obstacle that tries to discourage us and stand in the way of success. "Fear", then, is just another word for "problem". Think about it: if there were no such thing as problems in life, there would be no such thing as fear. What you have to do, then, in order to overcome your fear is to get the problem into the proper perspective. That way, you will see things more clearly and be able to figure out what you need to do. Let me give you an example.

Look at the following page. Study it for a second or two and tell me what you see … A black spot, right? Yes, but look again carefully. Can you see anything else (apart from the number at the bottom and the title at the top of the page, that is)? Most likely, you will say "No". But the fact is, there are also lots and lots of white spots. (Incidentally, I did type in lots of white spots, it's just that you don't see them as spots.)

The dictionary defines "black spot" as a dangerous or difficult place. On the previous page, the black spot is representative of a problem or difficulty which causes worry, anxiety and fear. What happens when such feelings occur is that we tend to focus on the problem — on the black spot — and become oblivious to everything else. When all we can see is the problem in front of us, it becomes very easy to let the problem (the fear) take control of us. This not only pulls us down, it also makes it very difficult to see a way through the trouble. By putting things into the proper perspective, by looking at the whole picture instead of just the black spot, we begin to see that things are never quite as bad as they may first seem. Once we grasp this truth, everything is put back into focus. Now, we can see the problem for what it really is: a tiny dot relative to the whole picture. Instead of the black spot being the focus of our attention, we can diminish its power over us, and concentrate on fighting the fear and taking action to overcoming the problem.

There is another common fear which often becomes a formidable stumbling block, standing in the way of success: it is the fear of making a wrong decision, otherwise known as procrastination. I shall cover this subject in my next letter, but for now I will leave you to mull over these words from William Shakespeare: "Our doubts are traitors, and make us lose the good we oft might win by fearing to attempt."

Let me paraphrase that by saying, "If you do the thing you fear to do, you stand a far better chance of success than by doing nothing at all."

Yours cordially,

Uncle Bob

CHAPTER NINE

Procrastination

Dear Go-getter,

IT WAS THE English poet and dramatist Edward Young (1683–1765) who first coined the well-known phrase, "Procrastination is the thief of time." To procrastinate means to put off, to delay or defer until later. The word "procrastinate" originates from the Latin word "procrastinare", which literally means to postpone until tomorrow (*pro* meaning "for" and *cras* meaning "tomorrow"). Of course, the problem with procrastinating is that, if you keep postponing things until tomorrow, tomorrow never arrives.

The fact is, our everyday lives are full of decisions or choices that we have to make. Sometimes we make the right decisions and sometimes we make the wrong ones, but that's life. As they say, "No one is perfect."

Often, people procrastinate because of the fear of making the wrong decision. Think about it: if every one of us was able to determine the outcome of a decision before we made it, if people were able to perceive exactly what would happen, then there would be a lot less procrastination around and, in its place, a lot more decisiveness. Alas, in the real world it doesn't work like that.

What we need to understand, then, is that success is achieved through failure. It is only by making mistakes and then learning from them that we eventually succeed. Consider, for a moment, a child taking his first steps. Does he procrastinate? Certainly, he does. And then, when he has eventually plucked up the courage and made the decision to let go and begin to walk unaided, does he fail? Of course he does, and many times, too — which is often a painful experience! However, eventually, through perseverance, the child succeeds in walking — he succeeds through failing.

Someone once said that if we waited until all the traffic lights were green before we set off on a journey we would never leave home. In other words, don't wait around for the time to be just right, because the time is never just right. Indeed, as someone else once said, "The right time and the right place is right now." Every once in a while, we have to take a chance, we have to take whatever information we have available to us and just run with it. Yes, we might make a few mistakes on the way, but remember that old adage, "The man who never makes mistakes never makes anything," or, to put it another way, "He who is faultless is lifeless."

Sometimes (note that I said "sometimes") it is better to make a wrong decision than no decision at all. When you procrastinate and keep putting off making a decision, you can end up worrying about it and wasting much valuable time literally getting nowhere fast. It's like being on a rocking chair: try as hard as you like, it won't get you anywhere. At least if you make the wrong decision you'll soon find out about it, and then you can do something constructive to rectify the problem and put things right. I once read the following wise words (attributed to O.A. Battista), which perfectly demonstrate this point: "An error doesn't become a mistake until you refuse to correct it." Now, isn't that so true? An error, or making the wrong call or a bad judgement, is only an irrevocable mistake if you refuse to correct it.

I remember recently giving some similar advice to "David S.", the director of sales and marketing for an international company. David had been considering two men for a position within the company, but he couldn't decide which of the two to choose. Both candidates wanted the job and each had comparable, yet different, skills, strengths and weaknesses. Because it was such a close call,

David was procrastinating over a decision that really needed to be made. He was also concerned that in promoting one man he would have to deflate the hopes and aspirations of the other. Basically, his procrastination was due to his fear of making the wrong decision. I told him that sometimes it is better to make a wrong decision than no decision at all, and advised him to go along with his gut feeling and make the decision immediately. He did and, although it was a bumpy ride for while, everything worked out all right in the end.

Being decisive and taking action is, I know, one of those things that is often easier to say than do. However, when you find yourself procrastinating and at a loss over what to do, search for that gut feeling. Weigh up the consequences of the decision, the points for and against, and ask yourself: Overall, would this decision be constructive or destructive towards my future plans? Then, either go for it or forget about it.

Benjamin Franklin, the American statesman, scientist, inventor and author, who was responsible in part for drawing up the Declaration of Independence and the American Constitution, had a very effective method for making decisions. He would simply take a piece of paper and draw a line down the middle to create two columns, which would be headed "For" and "Against". He would then proceed to list as many items as possible on either side of the paper. And when he had exhausted his supply of ideas he would simply add up the columns, and make his decision based on whichever column outweighed the other. Simple but effective. Benjamin Franklin was, without doubt, a very decisive man. He was also a man of many wise words, several of which he shared in his book of aphorisms and proverbs, *Poor Richard's Almanack*. Here is an example relating to procrastination: "You may delay but time will not … Lost time is never found."

Wise words indeed, but what should you do when the choice is not so clear-cut, when you really have no idea what to do? Well, in this situation, my advice is very simple and straightforward: pray about it and seek divine guidance. When Jesus taught his disciples how to pray, he said to them, "Ask and it will be given to you; seek and you will find; knock and the door will be opened to you."

(Luke 11:9) So, when you are searching for direction or you have a major decision to make, pray for guidance, believing that your prayers will be answered. Then, somehow, some way, you will discover what it is that you should do. You'll get an inclination or a sign, or that gut feeling that tells you which is the right road to take. When the answer is revealed, when you discover the way forward and you have that gut feeling that it's right, then don't fight it, don't doubt it and don't worry about it, just go along with it. Worrying about a problem doesn't do anything except make you miserable and, maybe, give you a few ulcers. Consider again the words of Jesus: "Who of you by worrying can add a single hour to his life?" (Matthew 6:27) Worrying, then, only creates doubt and fear and gets you nowhere fast — it's like being on that rocking chair again!

Of course, there is only one way to effectively deal with procrastination, and that is by taking action. You see, procrastination is not always so much to do with the fear of making decisions. Sometimes, it is more to do with taking action upon those decisions. In other words, people will often make a decision in their mind but then keep postponing or putting off taking the necessary action to implement the decision. As you know, I like to define the word "action" as putting our mental ACts (decisions) into moTION.

Action, then, as with all decision-making, involves an element of risk. No doubt you will have heard that other old adage, "Nothing ventured is nothing gained." That is the same as saying that if you don't take chances, or dare to risk, then you won't move ahead or achieve anything worthwhile. Consider this: just as tortoises only move forward when they stick their necks out, so we must also do the same. Remember again what Abraham Lincoln said: "Things may come to those who wait, but only the things left by those who hustle." If you procrastinate, delay, hesitate, postpone the decision or wait around for the problem to either solve itself or go away, then you've got a long wait ahead of you. And, meanwhile, success is passing you by. The internationally-acclaimed public speaker and best-selling author Dr Denis Waitley versed the following poem, which, although amusing, also has a serious message contained within it:

Opportunities Missed

There was once a very cautious man
Who never laughed or cried.
He never risked, he never lost,
He never won nor tried.

And when one day he passed away
His insurance was denied,
For since he never really lived,
They claimed he never died!

People who genuinely seek self-improvement and success are people who are willing to take risks. But taking risks is a dangerous business, which often involves making mistakes and getting hurt. However, this doesn't stop some people, especially not the winners in life, because they have come to learn and understand that success really is achieved through failure.

In conclusion, I want to admonish you again: do not succumb to procrastination, never put off until tomorrow what you can do today. Instead, be willing to take risks, be decisive, make your decisions and then have the strength of your convictions to take immediate action and implement those decisions.

Yours decidedly,

Uncle Bob

CHAPTER TEN

How to Overcome Failure

Dear Go-getter,

THERE IS, AS I have already mentioned, a universal truth which stipulates that sustained success can only ever be achieved through failure. In this letter, I want us to look at how to effectively overcome failure and get back on track again.

Every successful person, no matter who they are or where they come from, experiences failure before he or she succeeds. Failure is simply a part of the learning process — which, of course, helps us to grow. At the same time, failure also prepares us and ensures that we appreciate our success when it does eventually arrive. So, you see, failure is actually part and parcel of success. In a nutshell, you have to experience failure before you can experience and enjoy sustained success. Now, that doesn't mean to say that you have to embrace failure or accept it as being permanent. Rather, you must understand that it is inevitable, and learn how to deal with it.

We only have to look at history to see how the successful men and women of the past have had to endure and overcome many obstacles, setbacks and failures before they achieved success. Some famous examples are listed below.

♦ As a young man, Walt Disney was fired from his job on a newspaper because of his shortage of creative ideas. Then, as an entrepreneur, he was often flat broke, and went bust on several occasions before he eventually succeeded and went on to build Disneyland.

♦ Henry Ford, founder of the Ford Motor Company, is another success-achieved-through-failure story. He failed and went bust five times before he eventually made it.

♦ Ray Kroc was founder of the McDonald's fast-food empire. He was a 52-year-old salesperson earning $12,000 a year selling milk-shake machines, when he made a business proposition to the McDonald brothers. However, this was not so much an act of prudence as the act of a desperate man. You see, Ray Kroc knew that the milk-shake machines he was selling and the company he was working for were destined to fail because of superior competition from another firm. Ray Kroc, middle-aged, failing, but eager to survive, is reported to have said, "If I lost out on McDonald's I'd have no place to go."

♦ Colonel Sanders, of KFC (formerly Kentucky Fried Chicken) fame, began the fast-food chain with just a simple recipe for his "finger-lickin'" chicken. It has been reported that he trudged from one restaurant to another, trying to persuade the owners to use his special recipe and pay him for the privilege of doing so. Needless to say, he failed many times and received more than a few rejections. But then, eventually, someone took him up on his idea.

♦ Finally — love her or hate her — consider Lady Margaret Thatcher, who first ran for parliament in 1950 but failed to get elected. Unperturbed, she stood again the following year and, once again, failed to win the seat. Eight years later, in 1959, she attained her goal and was, finally, elected. Twenty years after that, Margaret Thatcher became Britain's first-ever woman Prime Minister. She was also the first woman in

Europe to attain such a position: another prime example of success achieved through failure.

Now, I'm not suggesting for one moment that I fall into the same category as any of the above examples but I have, in my own way, experienced much in the way of failure. I believe that others might be inspired by my story, and it is with this in mind that I now share some of my own personal details with you. Before I do, however, let me spell out clearly the message that I want to portray. And that is: despite your circumstances, regardless of your background and no matter what obstacles stand in your way, nothing, absolutely nothing, can withstand the sustained assault of hard work coupled with the will to win. Now, let me assure you that those are not empty words but words written with complete conviction. With my background, if I can achieve a considerable measure of success, then anyone can.

Briefly, you could say that I'm the product of a broken home, but not just one broken home — rather, several. You see, I know what it feels like to be abandoned; I was adopted at the age of three. I know what insecurity feels like; growing up, I knew four separate men as "Father" and yet I have never known what it is to have a father. I also know what it feels like to be rejected and have no friends; during my school years we moved house eight times and I attended four different schools.

Not surprisingly, I didn't enjoy school or succeed very much in the classroom, but nevertheless I did show some potential. At the age of 11, I sat what was then called the "Eleven Plus" exam, which determined whether or not a person would go to grammar school. I was a borderline case (meaning the examiners couldn't decide whether or not I had passed), so I had to send all my school-books off to the inspection board for evaluation. I failed and felt utterly dejected. In fact, my only happy memories of childhood come from living with my grandmother, which I did from the age of 12 until I left home at 18 to make it on my own.

So, you see, I know what failure is, I know what rejection is, I know what it's like to feel that your problems are insurmountable; and yet, through it all, even at such a young age I always had a deep-down desire to win, to prove myself, to rise above the limitations others imposed on me. And that's why I can say, with conviction, "Success is achieved through failure." At the end of the day, if I can do it, anyone can.

As I'm talking about belief, here is a poem (author unknown) that has often spoken to me, and one that I hope will inspire you to believe in yourself:

Believe In Your Ability

Doubt can stop you in your tracks,
It can drain away desire,
Believing, on the other hand,
Can set your world on fire.

When you hold the opinion that
You can reach that special dream,
You have the edge needed to make
Achieving much easier than it may seem.

Believing in your ability
Affects the way you act,
And produces an air of confidence
Which influences how others will react.

When you believe you can achieve
And believe it with all your soul,
You possess a powerful asset
And you'll most likely reach your goal.

Failure and defeat are obstacles standing in the way of success, but obstacles, for the most part, are not insurmountable. They may impede or hinder progress, but they don't actually stop it (not unless you allow them to). How, then, can a person effectively deal with failure and defeat? To answer that question, I've listed some ideas.

Ten ways to overcome failure and get back on track

1. *Look for the success in failure*

Nobody in their right mind enjoys failing, so when it does happen it is natural to feel upset. A good way to shake off despondency is to try to find some success in whatever it was that you failed at. You must have done something right. What was it? If you look hard enough you can always find something good and then, when you do, you'll see that things aren't really all that bad. In fact, when you analyse failure, you'll see that every defeat conceals success of some kind. So, you could say, "Failure is success dressed in disguise."

2. *Find the cause*

Let me ask you another question: If you were to learn a worthwhile lesson, would you consider that a positive or negative exercise? Well, then, use the experience of failure to learn a worthwhile lesson, to learn from your mistakes. There's an old adage that says, "Don't fix the blame, fix the problem." That means don't point the finger at someone else. (When you do this — point your finger at someone else — notice how there are always three of your own fingers pointing straight back at you. Try it.) Study the cause of failure, find out what went wrong, learn from your mistakes, then set out to rectify the problem by starting over.

3. *Consider things over time*

I once read that, when Thomas Edison died, among the papers on his desk was a note, scrawled in his own hand, which said, "When you're down in the mouth, consider Jonah — he came out of it all right." The point I'm trying to make here is that failure should not be looked at in the heat of the moment but, rather, over a period of time. When you consider failure over a period of months, or even years, it loses energy, and you will see that failure is only a temporary setback, not a permanent way of life. Your own personal failures can only derive as much power as you allow them to, so don't dwell on the moment; instead, consider things over time and discover afresh that failure is temporary. Then pick yourself up, dust yourself off and start over again.

4. *Use past success to diminish present failure*

Here, I am not so much talking about reminiscing about old war stories to create the feel-good factor — although that in itself can often be just the right tonic to overcome a failure. Rather, what I'm talking about here is something adapted from the profession of selling: using the law of averages to put failure into its proper perspective. In other words, concentrate on your overall percentages rather than momentary results. For example, suppose it takes a salesperson five calls in order to make a sale and earn a commission of $500. Using the law of averages, each call is, in effect, worth $100 (including the four rejections). Looking at it this way, every failure has earned the salesperson $100, and in the process he or she has also moved one step closer to making a sale. Once again, we can see that failure is not the end result, but merely a part of the success process.

5. *Count your blessings*

Whenever you're feeling down, when failure has drained you to the point of being sapped of all energy, just remember that worse things happen at sea! Failure isn't the be-all and end-all, it's just a hurdle in the race, a hurdle that slows you down. When I was a boy, whenever things weren't going my way, my grandmother would say to me, "Count your blessings." To count your blessings is to focus on the positive, to remind yourself of all the good things you have and to consider your every good fortune. For example, do you have good health? Can you see with your eyes and hear with your ears? Do you have a family, people who love and care for you? Do you have a job, a home, money in your pocket, a future? So, then, instead of feeling sorry for yourself, count your blessings and consider just how fortunate and how great a success story you really are. Get things into perspective.

6. *Create a positive resumé*

List on paper a complete record of all your positive attributes and qualities as if you were preparing an over-the-top personal resumé on yourself. Also include a record of all your accomplishments and achievements — anything you can think of — going back as far as you can remember. Start with your school-days and list every little success you can recall. If anything positive comes to mind, write it down. Once you have completed this exercise, you need to sit back for a moment or two and study the detailed record in front of you. In doing so, you'll rediscover what a truly magnificent person you really are, which, of course, is a great pick-me-up to boost your self-esteem and inspire you to get back into action again.

7. *Practice makes perfect*

If, in a particular situation, failure is inevitable, put the failure to good use by practising your techniques. Take the earlier example of running in a hurdles race. Now, in this particular race you're up against the Olympic champion and there's no way you're going to win, barring some unfortunate accident. But just because you're not going to win doesn't mean you have to fail. You can still try for second place, you can still try for a personal-best time or even just practise the technique of straddling the hurdles. Psychologist Dr Denis Waitley put it beautifully when he said, "Turn failure into fertiliser." To succeed and win at anything takes lots of training and practice. Failure gives you a perfect opportunity to do just that. Perfect your practices.

8. *Laugh in the face of adversity*

Don't take life so seriously. There's no question that this is a difficult one. It takes a lot of guts, and a special kind of character, to laugh in the face of defeat, and I don't even know whether I am qualified to be writing this. However, I have chosen to do so on the promise to myself that I must always practise what I preach. This one action — laughter — is the most effective way of not letting failure beat you.

Another important attribute of laughter is that it's contagious. (Remember those laughing boxes that you used to be able to get at the novelty shop when you were a child?) Sometimes you may have to force a smile to start with but, as soon as you do, that natural and contagious process takes over. It is just like the words of an old song: "Smile and the whole world smiles with you." Try it. Smile at someone, give them a big toothy grin and keep it going. Before long, they'll be smiling along with you and, if you keep at it, the end result will be spontaneous and uncontrolled fits of laughter. It has been rightfully said that, "A smile is a little curve that sets a lot of things straight."

9. *Don't take it personally*

Understand that, in business, it is not you as an individual that fails or is rejected. Rather, it is your product or service or company, or possibly the way in which you presented it — that is what's rejected. Sometimes you might have to force yourself to think along these lines but, when you do, you'll see the truth and you'll know that even though you might have done a second-rate job it wasn't you as a person, as a human being, that was rejected. If you did make a poor job of it, it's okay to be disappointed, and even self-critical, but make sure it's constructive criticism and not destructive criticism.

10. *Let go and let God*

Sometimes, you simply have to let go of your failure, forget about it and move on. The most effective way I know of doing this is through prayer. Peter, one of the disciples of Jesus, wrote, "Cast all your anxiety on him because he cares for you." (1 Peter 5:7) Hand over your anxiety and your failures, let go of them and let God deal with them.

Let me leave you with a final piece of advice on how to overcome failure: if at first you don't succeed, try, try again, and again, and again …

Yours cordially,

Uncle Bob

CHAPTER ELEVEN

The Danger of Complacency

Dear Go-getter,

IN CONTRAST TO my last letter, where we looked at failure, I now want to consider another obstacle, but from the opposite end of the spectrum: that of complacency.

First of all, I think it would be useful to define the word "complacency". The following witticism serves this point reasonably well:

Teacher: Johnny, what does apathy mean?

Johnny: I don't know, Miss, and I don't particularly care, either.

A more accurate definition can be found in the *Collins English Dictionary and Thesaurus*, where complacency is defined as: apathy, comfort, contentment, gratification, indifference, being pleased with oneself, self-assuredness, self-righteousness, self-satisfaction, smugness, and being unconcerned. Are you getting the message?

Complacency is both dangerous and costly: dangerous, because it lurks menacingly behind every little success; and costly, because yielding to it lulls you into a false sense of security. Often, after enjoying some success, people become complacent, and act as though they have arrived at their port of destination, when in fact they are still out at sea. (As indeed we always should be. Remember, success is the excursion itself, not a target or destination.) Revelling in the confidence of past accomplishments, these people say to themselves, "Hey, I've done it! I've arrived. I'm successful." Then they let up, drop anchor and begin to relax.

Now, at first glance it might appear that I am contradicting myself if I say that a little complacency is good for you. However, I would like to emphasise the point: a *little* complacency. In other words, feeling content and satisfied is not a bad thing, just as long as you're careful not to overdo it. Complacency, then, can also be defined as the "feel-good factor". It is good to pat yourself on the back, to relax and revel in our own achievements and success for a while. However, as we become more confident and self-assured we can, all too often, relax a little too much. It is here that we enter our comfort zone, which for some would be far better termed "the danger zone". You see, complacency is very, very comfortable, and this is what causes the problem. It can be so comfortable that people don't do anything about it until it's too late. Then, before they know what's really happened, their success is replaced with despair and despondency, which have sneaked up on them without them even realising it.

You will remember that a while ago I gave you an analogy about travelling in a hot-air balloon. I am going to repeat it to you again now, to remind you of the dangers of complacency.

Consider your journey of success, indeed your journey of life, to be like travelling in a hot-air balloon. To proceed on this journey you must continuously ascend to greater heights by applying the necessary fuel (that is, heating up the gas inside the balloon). It is okay to shut off the fuel supply every now and again, it's all right to feel a little complacent and admire the view for a time. After all, that's what a successful balloon journey is all about: being able to sit back every once in a while to relax and enjoy the view. And that is exactly what a hot-air balloon is designed to do. Once it's high enough, it will happily hang in suspension, or ride on the wind and air currents, for a while, at least. However, if you don't turn the fuel supply back on, if you sit back for too long revelling in complacency, then your hot-air balloon will start to cool down and, inevitably, you will start to descend. The descent is so gradual that at first it is hardly recognisable, but it doesn't take long to pick up speed. Indeed, many people get so carried away with the view that, instead of concentrating on remaining aloft and continuing to rise, they relax and fall into the illusion of having already arrived at their destination. Before they know what's hit them, their descent is out of control and they're falling so fast they can't slow down or stop themselves — not until they eventually come back down to earth with a bump.

So, first and foremost, understand that the key to a continued and successful journey lies in measuring the dosage of complacency and taking immediate and effective action as soon as you realise that you are suffering from too much of it.

The following fable further illustrates the point that too much complacency is very costly:

The story goes that one day the wise and learned old Tortoise challenged Hare to a race. Now, this would not normally be much of a race, as a hare can, obviously, outrun a tortoise. But, as I've already said, Tortoise was a very wise and learned fellow and, although he knew that Hare could outrun him, he also knew Hare to be a very complacent chap. Upon hearing the challenge, Hare fell about laughing, but then, after realising that Tortoise was serious, he accepted.

The route was decided, and the first to the finishing post was to be the winner. When the starter sounded, Hare set off at a roaring pace and left Tortoise standing in the blocks. After about a mile, Hare looked over his shoulder, but Tortoise was nowhere to be seen. Hare smiled to himself. It was a hot summer's day, so he decided to stop and rest for a while under the shade of an old oak tree. Hare, knowing the race was as good as won, and feeling more than a little self-satisfied, decided to take a nap.

Meanwhile, Tortoise plodded on and on. By and by, he came across Hare, who was now fast asleep in the shade of the big oak tree, and, without making a fuss, he quietly passed him by. When eventually Hare woke up, the sun was beginning to set. He became alarmed at how long he must have slept for, and wondered if Tortoise had overtaken him without him knowing about it. At full pace, Hare set off again and headed towards the finish, but as soon as the winning post came into view he saw Tortoise ambling across the line to win the race.

And the moral of this tale, once again, is that if we become over-confident and too self-assured we can also become too blasé, too casual, too relaxed, which is to say that we enter not so much the comfort zone as the danger zone. Yes indeed, complacency costs.

Here is another example of apathy at work, with the lesson this time being the very real dangers of allowing yourself to become complacent:

The story goes that down in that place called Hades, Satan summoned his three chief demons to a debate on how to win as many souls as possible for the Kingdom of Hell. After much discussion, one of the demons came up with an idea. "I know," he said. "How about I disguise myself as a mortal and go to earth proclaiming that there is no such thing as God or the Devil or Heaven or Hell? I'll tell everyone that there is no inherent good or evil and that the only thing that matters is self-gratification. That way, alcohol, drugs, gambling, promiscuity, debauchery and the like will no longer be taboo. I predict that I'll be able to secure the souls of up to half of the world's population."

Satan thought this was a wonderful idea and was just about to give it his approval when the second demon interjected. "I have an even better idea," he said. "I'll disguise myself as a mortal and go to earth, but I'll proclaim that there is a God and a Devil and that there is a place called Heaven and a place called Hell, so everyone had better go to church every

Sunday or else!" He then went on to say, "But then I'll tell everyone that, as long as they go to church on a Sunday, the rest of the week they can do whatever they like. That way, I reckon I could get the souls of three-quarters of the world's population down to Hell."

Satan was delighted, and rubbed his hands together with glee, but then the third demon piped up. "I have the best idea of all, and an idea that could get everyone on earth down to Hell." The whole of Hades fell silent as Satan nodded, beckoning the third demon to continue. "I'll disguise myself as a mortal and go to earth, and I, too, will proclaim that there is a God and a Devil and there is a place called Heaven and a place called Hell. I'll tell everyone that they must live clean and honest lives and follow the teachings of the Bible. But then I will also tell everyone that there's no rush, so they can take all the time in the world to think it over."

Once again, the moral of this little tale is that complacency is dangerous — in this case, eternally dangerous!

The blockbuster disaster movie *Titanic* serves as another example of the dangers of complacency, which in this case resulted in some 1,500 men, women and children losing their lives. You will remember that the *Titanic* was the ship that sank on her maiden voyage, in 1912, after hitting an iceberg. *Titanic* was considered by her owners, the White Star Line, and her insurers, Lloyd's of London, to be unsinkable. In fact, so complacent were they about *Titanic's* invulnerability that the ship was allowed to sail with only enough lifeboats for half the people on board. When the accident happened, at 11:40 p.m. on 14 April, there was very little in the way of commotion among the passengers, who were simply told that there was a minor problem which would cause a short delay. The ship's orchestra carried on playing, and passengers continued to socialise and make merry in the comfortable saloons.

When eventually the order was given to man the lifeboats, many passengers refused to leave the warmth and comfort of the ship's saloon, preferring instead to believe that the ship wasn't in any real danger. The thought of venturing out onto the icy, cold Atlantic Ocean in a lifeboat at the dead of night initially seemed preposterous to many passengers. Ironically, the first few lifeboats pulled away only half full, and the rest of the story, as they say, is history. Let me say it one more time: complacency costs.

Having now looked at the danger of complacency, let us move on and look at how to deal with the problem. Now, obviously, prevention is always far better than cure, but when complacency does take hold there is, really, only one cure, and that is to take immediate corrective action (just like reapplying the heat for our hot-air balloon). In other words, what I'm saying is that you need to do something to implement immediate change — change for the better, obviously. You need to get on the offensive instead of the defensive, because the only way to overcome complacency is to attack it head-on. So, don't wait around for things to get better by themselves, otherwise your descent will soon be out of control. Instead, make an irrevocable commitment to get into gear and move forward again. I sometimes like to put it this way: "You can't advance or get ahead when you're in neutral or reverse gear. To move forward again, you have to get into first, first."

To overcome complacency and get back on track again, you have to want to want. Yes, you did read that correctly: you have to want to want. Let me explain. (You might have to read the next two sentences slowly for them to make sense.) When you want to do something — I mean *really* want to do it — then there's nothing that will stand in your way, is there? To overcome complacency and get back on track again then, you have to want to want to do it — whatever "it" may be.

To create that desire, that "want", again, you have to coerce yourself out of your comfort zone and force yourself back onto the battlefield; back into the fight for survival. Remember what I said previously about burning your bridges? That's exactly what you have to do in this situation: burn your bridges, make an irrevocable commitment so there is no going back. Then, it is either do or die, sink or swim.

Dragging yourself out of your comfort zone and forcing yourself back into the survival zone is the only sure-fire way of curing complacency.

Let me leave you with some sage advice. In the words of Stephen R. Covey: "The most important thing is to make the most important thing the most important thing!" Don't take your eye off the ball. Instead, make sure that you make *the* most important thing *your* most important thing.

Yours cordially,

Uncle Bob

CHAPTER TWELVE

How to Deal With Despondency

Dear Go-getter,

A WHILE AGO, I said that I'd dedicate my next few letters to reminding you of certain issues or obstacles that stand in the way of success. In this, the last such letter before moving on, I want to look at how to deal with despair or despondency.

As I've said before, it's impossible to stay up on top of the mountain, on a "high" as it were, 24 hours a day, 7 days a week, 365 days a year. The plain fact of the matter is, what goes up must also come down! The first point that I want to establish, therefore, is that there's no shame in falling down, only in staying down!

Indeed, life is full of peaks and troughs — so much so, that one of the most important keys to sustained success is learning how to effectively deal with your times of despair and discouragement, learning how to pull yourself up by the boot-straps when you're downcast and disheartened so that you're able to rise up out of the rut and get back into action again. In this letter I'm going to share some more time-tested, time-proven methods that will enable you to deal effectively with that doom-and-gloom syndrome known as despondency.

In my earlier letters on "Self-Motivation" (Chapter 6) and "How to Overcome Failure" (Chapter 10), I listed some 22 different ways to help you turn your stumbling blocks into stepping stones! I'd like to recommend that you read these particular letters again, whenever you feel discouraged or despondent. This, really, is nothing more than good maintenance advice — like checking your car tyres, it makes good sense. To expand on that example, it allows you an opportunity to check your air pressure, plug any leaks and pump yourself back up again when you need to!

I said in my opening letter that it's almost as if discouragement were an invisible assailant prowling among the human race and attacking each and every one of us at every possible opportunity. As if it, discouragement, were some evil force whose only ambition was in sharing itself with as many people as possible and as frequently as it can, in order to keep them back and stop them from succeeding in life! One thing is for certain: wherever discouragement reigns, doubt was always the instigator!

Discouragement is like a toy balloon with a slow puncture, it gradually deflates a person and drains away aspiration and hope. If you allow yourself to listen to self-doubts, if you permit yourself to be affected by the negative influences that surround you, then discouragement will make you more and more despondent and continue to deflate you until eventually, you're totally spent.

In the literary classic, *The Pilgrim's Progress* by John Bunyan (1628-88), the story describes how the main character, Christian, travels through a place called, "The Slough of Despond" on his way to the "Celestial City". On his journey, Christian meets a man in an iron cage and inquires of him, "What art thou?" In response, the caged man answers, "I am now a man of despair, and I am shut up in it, as in this iron cage. I cannot get out, O now I cannot." The caged man then goes on to say, "I am what I was not once." That is such a vivid and accurate description of what despondency is like; an iron cage holding you prisoner.

Despondency is the iron cage that some animal trainers use to teach elephants to stay put and stop them from trying to escape. As an infant, the elephant is tied to a stake in the ground by securing a heavy iron chain around its foot. Try as it might, the young elephant is not strong enough to break the chain and free itself. Eventually, after many painful attempts, the elephant becomes so discouraged that it finally succumbs to despair and gives up, never to try again. From then on, even as a fully-grown adult measuring around three and a half metres in height and weighing up to four thousand kilograms, the elephant can be secured by only a thin rope and it will never again try to escape! (Too many painful memories!)

In reality, of course, a fully-grown elephant could very easily escape if it really wanted to but the fact is, the elephant is conditioned to think that it can't free itself and so it no longer bothers to try. In other words, the elephant doesn't know any better. It's often the same with people. Some people have become so disheartened and discouraged and so conditioned to failure that they succumb to despondency and give up trying. Now, of course, everyone gets discouraged and disheartened once in a while but not everyone gives up! When you do, despondency can and often does lead to depression. This I know from experience because I've been there myself, albeit a long time ago, and then for only a couple of months.

Ironically, before I started writing and speaking about issues on personal development and success, I too went through a period of depression. I will briefly describe it for you. At the time I was reaping the rewards of a very successful sales career and yet I felt discontented and somewhat disillusioned because I was no longer enjoying what I was doing. To some, it might have seemed as though I had everything and yet, I was dissatisfied and unhappy with life. The fact is, I was no longer doing anything that I considered to be fulfilling or worthwhile. True, I had achieved a great deal but then one day I discovered that I had lost my desire to work. I had money but I no longer had any goals. Instead, I was just living each day as it came, without any particular destination in mind, like that piece of drift-wood again, bobbing up and down on the ocean. I came to the awful realisation that a person becomes stale if their goals and present status are at one with each other, as mine were! So I quit my job and went home, with the intention of taking some time out, find myself again, to rediscover purpose, to gain new direction and seek new opportunities.

The fact is, however, that at the time I had no idea what a new opportunity would look like or if I'd even recognise it! The one thing I did come to rediscover, though, is that opportunity knocks only on the doors of those who go out seeking it and never on the doors of those who sit around waiting for it to come to them! Alas, I found myself doing just that. I sat around at home wallowing in self-pity and despondency as I tried to make sense of my predicament and find fresh purpose in my life! I would just mope about day after day, week after week, feeling more and more sorry for myself until eventually I really didn't care anymore. It was almost as if I was getting some sort of cynical pleasure out of feeling down, if that makes any sense!

Then one day I read a poem which so stirred me that I awoke from my stupor — and shortly afterwards, I discovered a new vocation and began writing. (By now, I'm sure you are aware that Edgar A. Guest is my favourite poet.) Here's the verse, by Guest:

How to Be Cheerful

How to be cheerful, do you say,
When the wind is cold and the skies are grey?
How to be cheerful? Just one way:
Forget yourself for awhile today.

Never mind self and your irksome cares.
Somebody else greater burden bears.
Stretch out a helping hand and play
The friend to all who may chance your way.

You'll never be cheerful sitting there
Sorrowing over the hurts that you bear,
For never a joyous hour is known
By the man who thinks of himself alone.

How to be cheerful? Scatter cheer;
Share your life with your neighbours here;
Encourage the weary and comfort the sad
And you'll find more joy than you've ever had.

My liberation from the depths of despair came about with the realisation that when you bend to help lift another to their feet, you can't help but lift yourself up at the same time. That statement is so important that it's worth repeating again: "When you bend to help lift another to their feet, you can't help but lift yourself up at the same time." I want to encourage you to adopt this disposition into your own personality because in doing so, you'll discover for yourself, it really is in giving that you receive.

Now, moving on, what else can a person do to effectively deal with despondency? Well, to start with, you have to want to change, I mean really WANT to change! The winners, in this game of life, are the people who, when they want to do something, stick at it until they succeed, no matter what! Such people internalise the old saying, "where there's a will there's a way." And winners find that way because they have the will for it, that is to say, they WANT "it" to happen, with a passion! On the other hand, however, when despondency sets in, especially through burn-out or lack of motivation, the problem lies in a person's lack of wanting, which can often lead to them giving up because they can no longer see the wood for the trees! When there's no fight left in a person, when they're burnt-out and redundant, then there's a very real danger that despondency will lead to depression. Understand then, that the first step to getting back on track is wanting it to happen, with a passion. And how do you do this? Here are some more suggestions;

1. *Get back to basics*

   What went wrong? What were your original goals? How have you become side-tracked? When you get back to basics and re-establish what it is that you really want, then you're well on the way to taking effective action. As Dr Robert H. Schuller says, "Beginning is half done!" So then, to get back on track, figure out what it was that you loved to do, then take a trip down

Memory Lane and do whatever it was again. Set yourself a new target, a new goal.

2. *Treat yourself*

    Whether it's a new toy, a new suit, a state-of-the-art computer or an exotic holiday — whatever it is, make sure it costs enough money to hurt your pocket, but without it putting you in a borrowing situation. This has a two-fold effect on dealing with despondency and getting you back into action. Firstly, your new toy or otherwise will create excitement, enthusiasm and that all-important feel-good factor to help motivate you. Secondly, in spending enough money to hurt your pocket, you'll also be creating an incentive to do something to repair the damage, to recoup your losses, as it were. Spending a significant amount of money, especially at such an unproductive time, will create fear. And fear is one of the most powerful motivators there is! (I am not condoning nor suggesting that you borrow money in order to treat yourself. Borrowing money may provide some short-term gratification but it could also provide some long-term misery, i.e. further despondency.)

3. *Score an easy point or two*

    For example, during sales training seminars I will often discuss "the sales slump". All salespeople, from time to time, hit the inevitable sales slump! Sometimes it's caused by the cylindrical wheels of commerce but mostly, a slump in sales figures is a result of a wrong attitude or despondency. To overcome this situation, I often suggest calling on a couple of regular accounts or looking to upgrade or sell more to an existing customer, etc. In other words, make an easy sale or two, whet your appetite again and, at the same time, regain some of that lost confidence. Once the wheels are in motion, the momentum picks up and gathers strength and then, in no time at all, you'll be climbing upwards again!

4. *Get it off your chest*

    For years, British Telecom have been running an advertising campaign with the message, "It's good to talk." And that's exactly what you should do — talk about it. As the saying goes, "a problem shared is a problem halved". So get it off your chest, talk to someone (find the right person), talk to yourself about it if you have to, but get it out of your system. You'll find that in doing so you help to clarify and, at the same time, diminish the problem.

It's been said that if you let the problems of yesterday die with the dusk then the opportunities of tomorrow will rise with the dawn. A good way of doing this is to write your problems out, spill the beans on paper. Then wipe the problems out by ripping the paper up and destroying it! The reasoning here is that in physically destroying your notes and disposing of them, you psychologically destroy and dispose of the problems in your own mind at the same time. And this, of course, enables you to refocus and concentrate once more on making things happen!

I believe in leaving the best until last. And so to finish off with, here's the best way to deal with despondency: prayer. I'll leave you with a verse of scripture, taken from Psalm 102, verse 17, "He [God] will respond to the prayer of the destitute; he will not despise their plea." (Brackets mine.) Now that's what I call reassuring!

Yours cordially,

Uncle Bob

CHAPTER THIRTEEN

Self-Esteem

Dear Go-getter,

AS WE'VE NOW tackled a dozen different attributes or characteristics to *maximise your potential* and enjoy lasting success, I'd like to look at the importance of self-esteem or self-image and, at the same time, briefly recap some previous points.

Feeling good about yourself — that is, having a positive self-image or high self-esteem — is such an important requisite that true success and happiness simply cannot be achieved without it. After saying that, however, liking yourself or having a good self-image is not such an easy attribute to acquire. The fact is, most people actually dislike themselves or at the very least, they dislike something about themselves. There is, unfortunately, a human tendency to dwell on such aversions, so much so that this often makes people fall short of their true potential. In other words, low self-esteem is primarily the culprit that causes most people to feel inadequate or incapable, and this in turn stops them from ever trying!

As I've said, high self-esteem is an essential ingredient for success. It's important to understand, however, that high self-esteem is not something that is simply inherited or acquired but rather, something that is developed over time and something that must be continually nurtured if we are to maintain it. As an example, although a somewhat biased one, I believe my children have what I would call high self-esteem. This, I believe, is partly because from the time they were born my wife and I have tried to shower our children with praise for their accomplishments. We've also tried to encourage them at every turn and have endeavoured to instil in them a sense of self-worth. Now, that's not to say that they or, indeed, other people with high self-esteem are immune to feeling inadequate or incapable every once in a while. Rather, people with high self-esteem are optimists who believe they have the capability to change things, to make a difference and to win, even when they don't come in first!

In this letter I shall be looking at how to develop and continually maintain high self-esteem. Before we start though, I would like to point out that high self-esteem does not mean that a person is egotistical or a show-off, nor does it mean that a person loves himself or herself to bits. That's self-importance, not self-esteem. There is a world of difference!

So then, to begin with, what I'd like you to do is assess your current level of self-esteem. A few years ago I devised a simple self-appraisal exercise that I sometimes use in my workshops. I've incorporated it below so that you can use it to appraise yourself. My reasoning here is not to get you to pass judgement on yourself or for you to be self-critical, but to get you thinking about how you really feel about yourself and to get you thinking about self-improvement. To that end, please answer the following questions, honestly! Remember, this is not a test but a self-appraisal exercise. (That means, don't try to pick the option that you think will give you the best score!) After reading the questions consider each of the four options carefully and then, even if the choices do not reflect exactly how you feel, select whichever option is *the most appropriate* one for you. Grab yourself a pencil before you start and put a tick by the letter corresponding to your answer. Here goes:

1. When you walk into a room full of people, maybe at a party or a seminar or business meeting, etc., how do you feel?

    a) Important, bold, possibly a little arrogant.

b) Insignificant, just one of the crowd.

c) Confident, self-assured.

d) Somewhat intimidated, as though everyone is looking at me.

2. Which of the following would you say best describes the way that you look?

a) I'm good looking.

b) I'm OK, fairly attractive.

c) I'm nothing special to look at.

d) I'm not good looking at all.

3. On the whole, which of the following best describes how lucky you are?

a) I'm lucky — I attract good luck.

b) I'm fairly lucky.

c) I'm unlucky.

d) I don't believe in luck.

4. How do you normally react when you experience rejection or a setback?

a) With a pinch of salt, there are plenty more fish in the sea!

b) I get depressed, it makes me feel despondent.

c) It frustrates me and makes me angry.

d) It upsets me but I try to learn from the experience.

5. How do you normally react when you receive praise or a compliment?

a) I reject it or say something to brush it to one side.

b) I accept it graciously and say thank you.

c) I become embarrassed.

d) I'm nonchalant and shrug it off as no big deal.

6. When you start something, a job, chore, project or maybe even a book, which of the following do you mostly tend to do?

   a) I stick with it until it's finished, regardless of distractions.

   b) I keep picking it up and putting it down until I eventually finish it, even though it may take a very long time!

   c) I am completely focused and give everything to the task at hand. I am only ever distracted if something more important crops up, but even then, I always return to finish the job.

   d) I always start with good intentions but never seem to be able to finish anything.

7. Let's suppose you wanted a raise in salary, what would you do?

   a) Look for another job with better pay.

   b) Ask the boss for a raise.

   c) Drop one or two subtle hints to the boss, implying that I'm underpaid and hope that he gets the message.

   d) Work harder with the attitude that I will earn my own increase in salary.

8. When you get dressed to go out to a special function, do you:

   a) Keep chopping and changing until you feel comfortable?

   b) Open your wardrobe and throw on the first thing you grab hold of?

   c) Consider beforehand what you are going to wear and stick with it?

   d) End up in a state because nothing feels right?

9. How often do you read or listen to non-fiction books, such as autobiographies, personal development, management or business books?

   a) Monthly or more frequently.

   b) About every three months or so.

   c) About once a year.

   d) Hardly ever.

10. In your job or whatever you do for a living, how would rate yourself as a competent or capable person?

    a) I consider myself very competent and I'm good at what I do.

    b) I'm reasonably competent and usually do well.

    c) I suppose I'm about average but I do okay.

    d) I don't consider myself to be competent or effective.

11. Which of the following best describes your disposition towards goal-setting?

    a) I live each day as it comes and don't really plan for the future.

    b) I've tried goal-setting before but it didn't work.

    c) I constantly set and review my goals, in writing.

    d) I'm ambitious and know what I want but I don't set goals, as such.

12. How do you normally react to having your photograph taken?

    a) I hate it!

    b) I'm not bothered, I don't mind it.

    c) I insist upon tidying my hair and showing my best side.

    d) I enjoy having my picture taken.

13. How often do you participate in an exercise routine or some form of physical workout to keep yourself in shape?

    a) Two or three times a week.

    b) Once a week.

    c) Once a month.

    d) Less than once a month.

14. When you consider your figure and your weight, which of the following best describes how you view yourself?

    a) I'm overweight and past caring. Nothing seems to work anyway!

b) I need to lose a few kilos but I'm okay.

c) I look and feel good and I'm happy with my weight.

d) I constantly worry about my weight.

Now using the following table, total your score and see how your self-image adds up!

1) a=3, b=2, c=4, d=1.
2) a=4, b=3, c=2, d=1.
3) a=4, b=3, c=1, d=2.
4) a=2, b=1, c=3, d=4.
5) a=1, b=4, c=2, d=3.
6) a=3, b=2, c=4, d=1.
7) a=2, b=3, c=1, d=4.
8) a=3, b=2, c=4, d=1.
9) a=4, b=3, c=2, d=1.
10) a=4, b=3, c=2, d=1.
11) a=2, b=1, c=4, d=3.
12) a=1, b=2, c=3, d=4.
13) a=4, b=3, c=2, d=1.
14) a=2, b=3, c=4, d=1.

Total score

14-21: If you fall into this category then you suffer from a very low self-esteem and most probably, you've often been miserable and depressed. To you, it must seem as though life is forever pulling you down, as though you always seem to draw the short straw! It's likely that you feel as though you never seem to have any energy; instead, you're weary and tired all the time, fed up with fighting yourself and others! The problem here is that your negative attitude and thoughts attract the very situation that you are trying to get away from. We really do become that which we think about, that which we imagine! Zig Ziglar puts it like this, "The most powerful nation in the world is your imagination!" At present you lack inspiration and hope, but take heart. As I said in my last letter, I was once in this situation myself and so from experience I can honestly say, it can and will get better, if you really want it to! Some people might respond to this comment with, "Yeah, that's all very well for you to say but my problem is different." However, the plain truth is, usually the only difference is in the way that a particular person views the problem! Before we move on to look again at ways of improving and maintaining high self-esteem, let me urge you not give up. Instead, be determined to change, to learn, to improve and remember no matter what, where there's a will there's a way! Remember also that "even through the thickest, darkest clouds the sun is still shining brightly!"

22-30: Mr Average! You have a self-image which is best described as mediocre. On a school report the teacher's remark would be, "Has the ability to do very well but needs to try harder." (Written in red for emphasis.) You have the potential but, more than anything else, you lack the desire to win. Here, I'm not talking about a passive want or wishful thinking but a real burning desire to improve and to win! You need to find purpose and remember that "success depends upon performance not potential!" Please read on.

31-39: You have a reasonably good self-image. You've been known to have your moments and have tasted success before. However, life is full of peaks and troughs and in this category there have definitely been more troughs than peaks. In order to reverse that trend you need to understand that "good luck is what happens when preparation meets opportunity" and that's exactly what you need to do right now, *prepare* yourself for future success by changing your attitude and improving your self-esteem. Adopting the techniques that are listed at the end of this chapter will help you to do just that.

40-48: You have a positive and healthy self-image. You have the ability, desire, determination and the potential to go all the way. However, sometimes, maybe you can be a little too stubborn, proud or possibly even over-confident and too full of yourself for your own good! In this category the biggest danger to self-improvement is yourself. That is to say, you either are or can be your own worst enemy! Remember that far too many people stop growing because they fall under the illusion of having already fully matured or arrived! They're now enjoying success, they feel pretty good about themselves, they're happy and consequently, they enter their comfort zone. This is where they stop learning and striving to improve and also, alas, where they inevitably begin to decline! Remember the old proverb, "When you're green you're still growing, but when you stop you start to rot!" Don't rest on your laurels. (According to the Collins English Dictionary, to rest on one's laurels is "to be satisfied with distinction won by past achievements and cease to strive for further achievements".) Don't do it, don't rest on your laurels, don't stop growing because you most definitely have got what it takes to go all the way!

49-56: You have a positive self-image and a great attitude. You're full of confidence and no stranger to success and yet you know that there will always be room for improvement. When you look into your own heart and mind, you like what you see, and so you should — you have the seeds of greatness! You also know that to attain greatness you have to continually maintain and nurture a positive self-image.

As I said earlier, the reason I have included the above exercise is not to get you to pass judgement on yourself or for you to be self-critical, but rather to get you thinking about your own self-esteem and also about self-improvement. Regardless of your score, what's important now is the future, not the past! And the future, your future, begins right now.

When all is said and done, the most important thing to remember is that success and happiness are not end goals or final destination points; rather, they are companions on our continuous journey of self-improvement. And, as with all journeys, every now and again you have to stop at a service station to re-fuel. (You have to take stock, to replenish and nurture your self-esteem.)

So why is high self-esteem or positive self-image so paramount to success? Well, for one thing, the person with high self-esteem has the most fun in the game of life. Let me give you an analogy to explain the point. Supposing you and I were to go out for a day at the races, say, horse racing at Flemington. We both have an amount of money to bet with, but let's say you have bundles and I have only a little. Now who do you suppose would have the most fun that day, you or me? That's right, you would! Because if you lost a few races it wouldn't clean you out and you'd still have plenty left to play with. I, on the other hand, would have to be far more cautious because I couldn't afford to take as many risks. With my small amount, I'd only have to lose a couple of races and I'd be out of the game altogether. That being the case, not only would I feel miserable at having lost what precious little I had to start with, but I'd also have to spend the rest of the day watching you having all the fun. It's the same in the game of life: the person with high self-esteem has the most fun because he or she can afford to take more risks. When they lose a race or two which, of course, every now and again is inevitable, they still have plenty of reserves left so it doesn't mean the game is over, just that the game changes direction slightly!

The main reason, though, why high self-esteem is the predominant factor for success, can be found once again in the acronym, WYSIWYG (What You See Is What You Get.) If you have a negative self-image and see yourself as a failure you will, ultimately, fail. On the other hand, if you see yourself as a winner, succeeding in life, you will do just that. Remember then, to visualise is to actualise — what you see really *is* what you get!

Before we move on to look at ways of how to develop, nurture and maintain high self-esteem, I'd like you to read and digest the following inspirational verse, which once again was written by the British-born and very talented Edgar A. Guest:

Equipment

Figure it out for yourself, my lad,
You've all that the greatest of men have had,
Two arms, two hands, two legs, two eyes,
And a brain to use if you would be wise.
With this equipment they all began,
So start from the top and say, "I can."

Look them over, the wise and the great,
They take their food from a common plate,
And similar knives and forks they use,
With similar laces they tie their shoes,
The world considers them brave and smart,
But you've all they had when they made their start.

You can triumph and come to skill,
You can be great if you only will.
You're well equipped for what fight you choose,
You have arms and legs and a brain to use,
And the man who has risen great deeds to do,
Began his life with no more than you.

You are the handicap you must face,
You are the one who must choose your place,
You must say where you want to go,
How much you will study the truth to know.
God has equipped you for life, but He
Lets you decide what you want to be.

Courage must come from the soul within,
The man must furnish the will to win.
So figure it out for yourself, my lad,
You were born with all that the great have had,
With your equipment they all began.
So get hold of yourself, and say, "I can."

To help you do just that, here are 15 different ways to develop, nurture and maintain high self-esteem. Some of these techniques I shall be mentioning here for the first time but others are principles that I've already explained in depth in previous letters. In the latter case, I'm repeating them briefly here, to serve both as a reminder and also as a way of summarising some of my earlier writings.

1. *Consider your worth*

Of the six billion people who make up the world's population today, and the countless billions who came before us, there has never been, nor will there ever be another person exactly like you. Realise then, that you are a unique being, a one-off creation, an absolute and complete rarity in the true sense of the word. You have your own thoughts, your own actions and your own preferences. You have unique gifts and abilities that are exclusive to you. It's true that many others have similar characteristics and abilities but no one else has precisely the same as you. You are indeed rare and, as is the case with all rare items, you have value. The fact is, you are the most precious, valuable commodity there is. Consider, for a moment, the miracle of your body... Your eyes and ears that allow you to see and hear God's wonderful creation, the world about us. Your arms, hands and fingers that allow you to touch, feel and create things in so many ways. Your legs, feet and toes that allow you to dance, walk, run and jump about. The list, quite frankly, is endless and when you meditate on such things, you'll see that your value is endless too. Consider your worth, then. How much are your legs worth to you? How much is your sight worth to you? How much is your life worth to you? Can a person put a price on such things? Absolutely not! Life is meant to be purposeful and priceless, not meaningless and worthless. The Bible tells us, "God created man in his own image." Appreciate then, that because you are so wonderfully made in the image of God, you are indeed priceless. After all, God doesn't make junk! Think about it. So then, to rebuild your self-esteem or when in times of dejection, count your blessings and put your worries into the proper perspective! Remember again, the words of Edgar Guest, "You were born with all that the great have had". So, "Get hold of yourself, and say, 'I can.' "

2. *Associate with the right people*

This has a knock-on effect. Simply put, the attitude of the "right people" will rub off onto you because the "right people" are enthusiastic people and enthusiasm is contagious. Enthusiasm is caught, not taught. Associating with the right people, whether through books, videos, cassettes or in person, will have a wonderful effect or your own self-esteem because you can't help but feed off them.

3. *Avoid negativity*

For the same reason as above — it's contagious. You'll, no doubt, have heard the expression, "Bad news sells good press". Why is it that newspaper sales and TV ratings always increase when there has been a disaster? Why is it that some of the best-read pages in newspapers and magazines are the Agony Aunt columns or problem pages? Is it that the readers are looking to be elevated by comparing themselves with the less fortunate? Could it be that they receive some sort of cynical pleasure from the tribulations of others? Or maybe they are hiding away from their own reality by getting lost in someone else's? Whatever the reason for their popularity, stay away from the problem pages and stay away from negativity. Avoid it like the plague because there's absolutely no good in it at all! Now, I'm not suggesting that you stop reading newspapers or watching the TV but rather, you should be selective. Just as you should be careful about what you eat and allow into your stomach, so you should also be careful about what you read or watch and allow into your mind. Some people say they're in control and capable of filtering out the bad stuff, but to that I say, "Nonsense!" If you eat bad food you get food poisoning and if you listen to problems, negativity, bad news and the like you end up with low self-esteem caused through mind poisoning. You simply cannot filter what goes in to the subconscious mind. Remember, Garbage Input Garbage Output. The same applies if you constantly listen to other people's gripes and moans. Listening to other people's excuses, problems and general negativity is like drowning in quicksand. People who are sinking will often try to pull others down with them, believing that they will find safety in numbers! In other words, in pulling you down to their level they pull themselves up to yours. So be warned, stay away from negative people and situations and protect your self-esteem.

4. *Think positive*

   Remember, our mind works like a magnet to attract that which we think about, be it positive or negative. Remember also what I indicated to you in a previous letter (Chapter 7), about how a piece of steel when it's magnetised (positive) is capable of lifting about twelve times its own weight, but when it's demagnetised (negative) it can't pick up a thing! It's the same with us, if we're positive, switched on, magnetised, then we can accomplish great feats but if we are negative, switched off, demagnetised, then we will accomplish nothing! So think positive and switch yourself on.

5. *Visualisation and auto-suggestion*

   To increase your self-esteem recall again, the four-step formula to condition your mind for success: Prayerise — Lift your requests to God. Visualise — In your mind's eye, see your petitions as having already been answered. Verbalise — Repeat positive affirmations to yourself. Materialise — Expect the results to actualise and wait patiently for them. (Refer again to Chapter 7, "The Powerful Force of Positive Thinking".)

6. *Dress up and go up*

   Remember when you dress up your attitude goes up. So to increase and build your self-esteem, make an effort to look smart by dressing up, polishing your shoes, getting a haircut, having a manicure, etc. When you look good you feel good, so make the effort and reap the rewards.

7. *Think big, act big*

   Following on from the above, another way to increase self-esteem is to act like the important person that you are. In other words: be different, be important, be special. Once again, we become that which we think about, so think big and act big (that doesn't mean arrogant), and you will indeed grow in stature, confidence and self-esteem. Let me give you a few examples of what I'm talking about:

   ♦ *Walk tall* — Keep your posture straight and walk more quickly. Let the world know and at the same time, see yourself as a person with a mission, a person who is going places!

♦ *Sit up* — The same applies when sitting. Everyone notices and pays attention to the person who is sitting up straight or has an elevated posture about themselves. (This is the reason why many manager's chairs are often higher than the ones at the opposite side of the desk! So that the manager can dominate his/her captives and ensure they pay attention.) Learn to adopt the posture of sitting up straight, rather than slouching. To do this, imagine that someone has the palm of their hand pushing against the small of your back.

♦ *Take the prime position* — Whenever there is a gathering of people, most try to sit as far away from the centre of attraction as possible, so that they don't draw attention to themselves. You should do the opposite and sit in the front row or nearest the stage. Be confident, think big, act big and become big in self-esteem.

♦ *Maintain eye contact* — If you find it difficult, force yourself to do it because keeping eye contact is one of the best ways I know of increasing confidence and self-esteem. Besides which, eye contact shows people you are sincere and that you are interested in them.

♦ *Speak up* — Whenever an opportunity arises you must speak up publicly. Most people just sit there and say nothing for fear of making a fool of themselves but you must overcome this fear. Remember: "if you do the thing you fear to do, the death of fear is certain". If you want to stand out from the crowd, if you want to be different, if you want to succeed and climb above the masses, then use your voice and speak up! Oh sure, sometimes you might be nervous and your voice might falter a little but don't let that deter you from persevering. Remember, persistence conquers resistance.

♦ *Always use positive communication* — Whether you're talking or writing always use positive language, because to maintain high self-esteem you need to talk the talk, as well as walk the walk!

8. *Start on the bottom rung of the ladder and take it one step at a time*

If you've been through some tough time which has left your self-image in tatters and your confidence shot, then this one is for you. Remember, Rome wasn't built in a day. In actual fact, the mighty city of Rome took many years to build and it all happened one brick at a time. And that's what you need to do, rebuild your self-image by taking things one step at a time. Start with a simple task, one in which you know you will succeed, then move on to another and another and another. With each step you'll grow in strength and confidence. It's like many small streams; eventually they converge and join together to become a mighty flowing river.

9. *Do it right and finish the job*

Take pride in whatever you do. Live by that old adage, "If a job's worth doing it's worth doing well." (And if it's not worth doing, why bother starting it in the first place?) There is no greater sense of satisfaction than knowing that a deed has been done well. And there is no better way of building self-esteem than taking pride in work that has been well done.

10. *Stand out from the crowd*

Be bothered enough to try and make a difference, to go the extra mile in everything you do and with everyone you meet. I intend to write further on this subject in a little while but for now, suffice for me to say, it's the little things that make a big difference. Here's a story as an example of someone who bothered to make a difference:

> Legend has it that several hundred years ago, in the heart of rural England, there lived an old man who had lost his entire family to the plague. Too old to start

again, the man knew that his family name would die out with him and that he would soon be forgotten about. It would be as though he had never existed at all. Saddened by this prospect, the old man decided to leave a legacy for future generations to enjoy. Something worthwhile, something that would make a difference, something to show that he had lived, even though he would always remain anonymous and never see the fruits of his labour. It is said that for the remaining years of his life the old man travelled around the countryside, moving from one village to another, planting acorns along the way. Whenever he saw a likely spot, where he imagined future generations would enjoy some shade, he would plant maybe a dozen acorns, knowing that possibly only one or two would grow to maturity. And when he was out in the meadows and came upon a magnificent oak with fruit too abundant to carry away, it's said that he would stay under the tree for a few days and plant the surrounding area until the supply of acorns dried up. Tradition has it that today many of the fine English oaks surrounding the villages and some of the dense oak woods and forests that still exist are the old man's legacy that he left for future generations to enjoy. (Maybe his seed did pass on after all!)

So then, to increase your self-esteem be bothered enough to try and make a difference, to go the extra mile in everything that you do and with everyone you meet. If you endeavour to make a good and lasting impression on the people you come in contact with you'll make a good and lasting impression on you — your self-esteem, that is.

11. *The power of prayer*

Those who believe and have faith know that there is nothing in this world as powerful as prayer. Nothing! Jesus said, "According to your faith will it be done to you." (Matthew 9:29) Likewise, Jesus also said:

> "If you have faith as small as a mustard seed, you can say to this mountain [*or problem*], 'Move from here to there', and it will move. Nothing will be impossible for you." (Matthew 17:20 — italics mine.)

What a promise! Nothing is impossible or unattainable if you have faith and put your trust in God. Let me say it one more time: there is nothing in this world as powerful as prayer. When you come to faith and you understand this truth, your self-worth takes on a whole new meaning! In a nutshell, when you come to understand that you matter to God, you also come to understand that no matter what problems you have, nothing is too big for God to handle! So pray, and have faith.

12. *Smile and increase your self-esteem*

I know that sometimes it's hard to smile but the truth is, it's actually easier to smile than it is to frown! Biologists have calculated that it takes 72 muscles to frown but only 14 to smile. So, even though it might not feel like it sometimes, it is in actual fact more than five times easier to smile than frown! Besides which, it has also been scientifically proven that smiling at someone not only makes the recipient happier but also makes the giver of the smile happier too. So smile, cheer up someone else's day and cheer up your own while you're at it. Someone once said, "Of all the things you wear, your expression is the most important." (Attributed to Janet Lane.) I agree, but would also add that we should wear a smile and not wear out a smile. That is to say, don't walk around with a permanent grin on your face. (Incidentally, being able to laugh at yourself, at your own mistakes, is another great tonic for self-esteem.)

13. *Take out your positive resumé*

Remember I suggested you list on paper a complete record of all your positive attributes and qualities as if you were preparing a personal resumé for yourself? (Refer to Chapter 10, "How to

Overcome Failure".) Now is the time to take it out and re-read it again, recalling to mind all your positive attributes and past achievements and reminding yourself just what a truly magnificent person you really are. This is exactly what your positive resumé was created for.. To act as a pick-me-up, a tonic to boost your self-esteem and inspire you back into action again.

14. *Set new goals*

I've already discussed this subject in depth (see Chapter 4, "The Meaning of Life") but I'd like to remind you that "if you fail to plan you plan to fail". Think about it for a moment. Imagine what would happen to a company like Microsoft if they didn't have any goals. At the end of the day, whether it's one of the world's largest companies or an individual person, goal-setting works! So become focused again and draw up a new plan of action. It always feels so much better when you know where you are heading and have a map or plan to follow.

15. *Help yourself by helping others*

Remember the echo effect or the boomerang principle: you always get back what you send out. Remember also, that when you bend to help lift another to their feet, you can't help but lift yourself up at the same time. So, to build and increase your self-esteem look towards offering a helping hand to others.

Well, we've now travelled quite a way together but so far to date, I have concentrated the majority of my efforts on writing about subjects primarily to do with vocation and the attributes needed to sustain success. Now, I'd like to move on to discuss matters of a more personal nature, stuff that helps to build character, a happy home, a loving family and a joyful, healthy life. My next few letters, then, will be devoted to these such subjects. So, until next time, I remain,

Yours cordially,

Uncle Bob

CHAPTER FOURTEEN

Habits – Make or Break

Dear Go-getter,

I SAID THAT I would dedicate my next few letters to more intimate matters and in this letter I'm going to be looking at habits; how to form good habits and how to break bad habits. It's often been said that we, as human beings, are creatures of habit which of course is very true.

Each and every day of our lives we succumb to thousands of habits, some good, some bad and some indifferent. For example, we eat at a certain time, we sit in a particular chair, we drive an identical route to work each day, we use the same petrol or gas station and so on. The list is endless, but the fact remains that we all perform many thousands of behavioural habits every day and for the most part, we are not even aware of it! Habits require very little, if any, conscious thought to perform. For example, our bodily functions such as breathing or sleeping, which are also habitual, require no conscious thought at all (these are obviously good habits!).

Habits are not formed overnight, but rather they are behaviours or acts that we grow accustomed to over time. In fact, some people get so accustomed to some bad habits that they become harmful. I've known smokers who love to smoke so much, especially with a drink or after a meal, that they would rather go without the drink or meal than go without a cigarette. I've known people who love to chew their fingernails, so much so, that they would often make their fingers sore. I've known drinkers who enjoy their habit so much that they intentionally go out to get inebriated. And I've known people who have used so-called "social drugs", which has resulted in the loss of lives. Indeed, some habits can literally become too close for comfort.

We are truly creatures of habit but, of course, they are not all bad habits. What I'm going to suggest is that you literally use this truth to your own advantage. You see, in this game of life, there's an unwritten rule that we must follow if we are to continually strive for personal development and success. I call it the MOB rule (Make Or Break) — meaning that we must continually develop or make good habits and at the same time, break or get rid of any bad habits.

On the wall of my study I have a framed picture of a magnificent eagle which, in full flight, is plucking a fish out of a lake. Under the picture is the following caption, *"We are what we repeatedly do. Excellence, then, is not an act but a habit."* How very true that statement is! Excellence is a habit, so is success and so is having a positive attitude and outlook on life. However, after saying that, there are always two sides to a coin and unfortunately, failure can also be a habit too! So then, whether it's success or failure, we are what we repeatedly do, we become that which we constantly think about.

Obviously, when it comes to bad habits prevention is always better than cure. As Benjamin Franklin once wrote, " 'Tis easier to prevent bad habits than to break them." The reason why it's so difficult to break bad habits is because they are so deeply rooted. In the simplest of terms, habits are things we become familiar and comfortable with. To change our habits or to form new habits means simply that we have to become uncomfortable, for a while at least, until our new behaviour becomes accepted and familiar to us.

Generally speaking, we all have at least some bad habits and most of us know what those bad habits are! Whether it's an obsession, fixation, addiction or some other detrimental behaviour pattern such as lateness, over-eating, impatience or careless driving, we know that such habits are wrong and in some instances harmful. For most part, people know that they really should do something about their bad habits. However, the fact is in many cases, they are just so comfortable with the habit that to deprive themselves the pleasure, relief or even apathy that the habit provides, is just too high a price to pay! In other words, people submit to instant gratification, short-term pleasure and listlessness because their desire to kick the habit is not as strong as their desire to continue with it. Often people will say they don't have the will power (to quit smoking or drinking or to diet or exercise, etc.), but what these people are really saying is that they don't have enough desire to change or quit the habit. In effect, they give up and accept defeat without putting up a fight!

On the other hand, however, the winners in life are people who, above all else, have determination. Winners have a cast iron will, a solid resolve to improve and succeed, and not just in business but in every area of their lives. It's this determination that guarantees them success! The fact is, it's not easy (winning anything worthwhile never is); if it were then everyone would succeed in everything they ever did! The truth is, to become is to overcome! And that takes guts, determination and hard work. I'm reminded here of a quote from the internationally-renowned, British hair stylist and entrepreneur, Vidal Sassoon. Here's a man who knows success through hard work. In a BBC radio broadcast he once quoted one of his school-teachers as saying, "The only place where success comes before work is in a dictionary."

So then, whether you resolve to make or break a habit, the first thing you must do, is accept that it's not going to be easy! There is no magic formula, there is no secret potion or medicine that will do all the hard work for you. It simply comes down to resolve, endurance and stickability! Once again, the key to success can be found in the maxim, "persistence conquers resistance".

Many of the subjects that I've previously written about, (continued learning, goal-setting, attitudes of the mind, etc.) are behavioural patterns or habits that can be formed or created. I'd now like to show you how you can do this; how you can form a new habit or to break an old habit over a period of 28 days or four consecutive weeks.

Throughout my adult life I have strived and indeed, continue to strive, for self-improvement using a formula that I discovered some years ago. I call the formula "MADE IT — 28". (This acronym stands for Make A Determined Effort — Invest the Time for 28 days, or 4 consecutive weeks.) If you'll do this, if you will make a determined effort to change or adopt a new behavioural pattern for 28 consecutive days, then you really will have made it! You'll have formed a new habit, a new behavioural pattern that your inner self accepts as normal because the new behaviour now feels comfortable.

Allow me give you one or two examples of how I've used the "MADE IT — 28" formula to successfully make and break some habits in my own life. Several years ago, after umpteen failed attempts over as many years, I finally kicked the habit of smoking. (In fact, it was this event that formed the foundation for my success formula.) Previously, my attempts to stop smoking had failed mainly for two reasons:

1. To stop smoking forever, always seemed too daunting a task or too long a time to deprive myself from doing something that I enjoyed doing.

2. After fighting the craving for three or four days I would reason with myself that having done so well and gone such a long time, I had proven that I could give up smoking whenever I wanted to. After that, it didn't take long for the inner voice of temptation to suggest that from now on, it would be all right to just have the occasional cigarette every once in a while, but only if and when I really felt like one. (Anyone who has ever smoked knows what happened next!)

Then one day I had an idea. Instead of looking at things long-term, i.e. stopping smoking forever, I would take a short-term view, just like short-term goal-setting. (Remember, short-term goals inspire and motivate a person to succeed because the results are almost immediate; whereas long-term goals, because there is no immediate gratification or reward, are rarely worked for with the same intensity and so consequently, they are often dropped or forgotten about.) I decided that I would set myself a short-term goal, I would stop smoking for 28 days and then, and only then, would I review the habit. I determined that if I wanted to continue smoking after the 28-day period, then I would. But, no matter what, for the next 28 days I wouldn't smoke a cigarette, not even if my life depended on it! Well, you already know what happened four weeks later but let me tell you, it was far from easy. In fact, the first few days it was very difficult, and then it got worse! After the first week, I was convinced that I would be smoking again at the end of 28 days and even had a packet opened and ready to celebrate the forthcoming event! Then, about half-way through the second week, I can remember feeling surprised that I had gone a whole morning without feeling the craving for tobacco. By the end of the third week, I was discovering new tastes and smells and already, I was contemplating extending the deadline for possibly another 28 days! Finally, by the end of the forth week, the habit was well and truly beaten — but not quite dead! As the saying goes, "old habits die hard". The truth is, after the 28 days it would have been the easiest thing in the world to go back to the old habit... but there again, it was just as easy not to!

Here's another example of personal success, using the "MADE IT — 28" formula. This time, the example is in forming new habits. Some years ago, I weighed in at 85 kg which is 190 lbs or 13.5 stones and, as I rarely did any form of exercise, I was not what you would call, physically fit. (When trying to kick a bad habit, it's good advice to fill the void or to substitute the bad habit with another behaviour, e.g. chewing gum instead of smoking. Unfortunately, in my case, I replaced one bad habit, smoking, with another bad habit, over-eating!) Anyway, using the formula, I dieted and exercised for 28 consecutive days. At the end of that time I not only saw results and felt much better but more importantly, I'd formed two new habits: being conscious of what I was eating and taking regular exercise. After only 28 days, these new behaviours had become so much a part of me, that if for some reason I didn't do them or I were to let up, I'd feel uncomfortable to the point of feeling guilty. So I did the only thing I could do, I continued with these new habits and, indeed, still retain them today. Over a period of time I lost 13 kg or 28 lbs in weight and (give or take a few pounds) that weight has stayed off, due mainly to my exercise routine. Originally, I set myself a short-term goal, in that I would exercise by jogging every other day for 28 days. Now, years later, the habit is so ingrained, so comfortable that it has become a living part of me. The simple truth is, I now love to jog and no matter where I am in the world, no matter what the weather is like, I try to go running at least three times every week. It doesn't matter if I'm feeling tired or I'm under the weather, I'll still go for my run and if, on occasions, I fall short one week, then I try to make up for it the next. Truly, I am a creature of habit.

Over the years I've used the "MADE IT — 28" formula to break a few bad habits but I've used the formula much more to create good ones. As I said earlier, the key ingredient to making the formula work is determination. The formula again, is not to Make An Effort (M.A.E.) but to Make A Determined Effort (M.A.D.E.). Here are the three steps you need to follow:

Step 1. *Don't delay, start today*

You'll most likely be familiar with the popular phrase, "Never put off till tomorrow what you can do today." Unfortunately, many people do not heed this sage advice and the result, of course, is procrastination and ultimately, failure. The fact is, procrastination is one of the most tragic causes of failure because the person who keeps putting off till tomorrow always finds that tomorrow becomes today too soon! Understand then, that the hardest part of doing anything is getting started! Dr Robert H. Schuller, author of the best-selling book *Tough Times Never Last But Tough People Do!*, puts it this way: "Winning starts with beginning." We begin by setting a goal or making a plan of action and then sticking to it. As someone else once said, "A goal properly set is already halfway achieved."

Step 2. *Concentrate on one step at a time (two as an absolute maximum).*

That is to say, focus on making or breaking only one or two habits at a time. Any more and you could find yourself choking to death because you have bitten off more than you can chew. In ancient

Rome, once the richest and most successful city in the world, there was a Latin proverb which, years ago, was translated into English and is still around today. I've quoted this proverb before but because it's relevant to our topic, here it is again: "Rome wasn't built in a day." In other words, you simply can't create a dozen new habits and get rid of all your old bad habits in one go. Permanent and worthwhile change takes place over time with one success leading to another and then another. Some 2,500 years ago the Chinese philosopher, Confucius, wrote, "A journey of a thousand miles begins with one step." And that's what you should do, start today and concentrate on one step at a time.

Step 3. *Strengthen your resolve by seeking support*

Once you have decided upon your 28-day programme, seek the support of loved ones or maybe a superior at work, somebody who will encourage you. Make a promise, to someone you would never let down, maybe a spouse or a child or Almighty God. Give whoever it is your solemn oath to stick with it for the 28 days no matter what. (Now you'll have to do it, otherwise you'll be going back on your word and you'll become a liar and a cheat!)

In conclusion, let me encourage you to continue striving for success and self-improvement by abiding to "the MOB rule". (Making good habits and/or breaking bad habits) and by using the "MADE IT — 28" formula. Understand and appreciate that this is not meant to be some sort of amusing play on words or a catchy slogan but a serious and proven method for self-improvement. (The anagrams were devised simply as a means of remembering the formula or guidelines.) At the end of the day, words are not important, action is what counts!

Let me leave you with a great little composition that I came across a while ago. I'm afraid that the original author, title and source are all lost to me. However, I have taken the liberty of adapting the prose slightly and if I could give it a title, I'd call it, "Good Habits of a Lifetime".

If you open it, close it.

If you turn it on, turn it off.

If you unlock it, lock it up.

If you break it, admit it.

If you can't fix it, find someone who can.

If you borrow it, return it.

If it's valuable, take good care of it.

If you make a mess, clean it up.

If you move it, put it back.

If it's not yours, get permission before you use it.

If you don't know how it works, ask first or leave it alone.

If it's none of your business, don't interfere.

If it isn't broken, don't try to fix it.

If it will encourage or inspire someone, say it.

If it will tarnish someone's reputation, keep it to yourself.

If you make a mistake, admit to it, make amends and move on.

If you receive more than you should, be honest.

If you drop it, pick it up.

If you take it out, put it back.

If you start it, finish it.

If you give your word, keep it.

If you can do it today, don't put it off.

If there's a queue, wait your turn.

If it's a worthwhile cause, be charitable.

If it's recyclable, don't throw it away.

If you ask or receive, use your manners.

I heartily endorse these principles and highly recommend that you adopt them, if you haven't already, as your own habits for a lifetime!

Yours cordially,

Uncle Bob

CHAPTER FIFTEEN

Stand Out From the Crowd

Dear Go-getter,

WHAT IS IT that causes the real winners in life to stand out from the crowd? Why is it that some people seem to be able to attract the "good things" in life? Is it just down to attitude? The answer is yes and no! Most certainly, attitude is a major contributing factor, but there is also something else, something much deeper than attitude.

I define it like this: The real winners in life are always completely dedicated to making a difference, however great or small, and it's this dedication that really causes them stand out from the crowd. Also, those individuals who attain true success and happiness always seem to have a certain aura about them, a belief, confidence, faith ... call it what you will. But there is, most definitely, an energy about them that is best observed in their attitudes and behaviour, especially towards others. In every case, it seems that these individuals are totally committed to service, to helping and improving the lives of other people. Could it be that simple? Could it be that in seeking to help others, the real winners in life inadvertently help themselves, so to speak?

In this letter, my aim is to reveal the truth behind this "secret of attraction", to show you just how it works and at the same time, hopefully, convince you to adopt and employ this powerful secret in your own life. However, in sharing this secret with you, there are two things I would ask. Firstly, that you actually use the information I'm about to give you. Don't just read it and put it to one side — instead, absorb it, adopt it and live by it! Secondly, that you share this secret at every opportunity you get, with anyone who will listen. Will you do that? Will you commit yourself to making a difference, however great or small? I hope so.

Finally, before disclosing this secret to you, I need to forewarn you that this concept I'm about to explain is very simple. I say "forewarn you" because it is so simple most people don't take it seriously; instead, they contemptuously disregard it or dismiss it as not being important. Here it is then, the secret of standing out from the crowd, the secret to lasting happiness and success... *"Treat people as you would really like to be treated."*

That's it! I said it was a simple concept and it is! Yet hidden in the above statement is real power. (Try reading the statement again, slowly this time, giving emphasis and meaning to each individual word.)

Now when I say, "Treat people as you would really like to be treated", I'm not just talking about being friendly, polite or courteous, as important as these things are. What I'm talking about goes a lot deeper than that. Let me put it this way. Imagine that you were introduced to someone that you really admired, someone you liked and respected, how would you like them to treat you? Certainly, you'd want them to be friendly, polite and courteous, but wouldn't you really want them to treat you as someone special? Wouldn't you really want that person to acknowledge you as an individual, to show a personal interest in you, maybe pass you a sincere compliment or share a word or two of encouragement or gratitude? Wouldn't it be wonderful if that person went out of their way, for no other reason than to make you feel appreciated and wanted? In other words, if they treated you *as you would really like to be treated*. That's what I'm talking about, treating a person how we all *really* want to be treated, as someone who is special, someone who is cared for, someone who is appreciated.

This is what Jesus of Nazareth meant some 2,000 years ago, when he gave the sermon on the mount and instructed us to "Do to others what you would have them do to you." (Matthew 7:12) Indeed, there is profound wisdom and power behind this simple instruction and yet, as simple as it may sound, so very few people grasp the meaning behind it. Basically, the hidden truth is found in this paradox: to give is to receive. Now, that's not to say a person should give in order to receive — that would be nothing more that an act of selfishness! Rather, we should give of ourselves for no other reason than our genuine desire to make a difference, however great or small. Those who come to understand this principle are the ones who really do stand out from the crowd, for they discover the secret of true success and happiness in life, that is to serve!

Among my archives of research and training materials collected over the years, I recently re-discovered the following verse (author unknown) which reverberates this instruction to treat people as you would really like to be treated.

Success

> *Success is speaking words of praise,*
> *In cheering other people's ways,*
> *In doing just the best you can,*
> *With every task and every plan,*
> *It's silence when your speech would hurt,*
> *Politeness when your neighbour's curt,*
> *It's deafness when the scandal flows,*
> *And sympathy with other's woes,*
> *It's loyalty when duty calls,*
> *It's courage when disaster falls,*
> *It's patience when the hours are long,*
> *And perseverance all along.*

Often people can be somewhat sceptical about this "to give is to receive" philosophy, and to them I simply say, try it out and see for yourself. Use the following approach for 24 hours, and I promise you, not only will you feel terrific about yourself, but you'll also be amazed at how people will react and at the results you will achieve. Try it for one day, be particularly nice and treat everyone you meet as someone who is really special. A word of warning, however: the key to making this secret work is sincerity. You have to be sincere in all your actions and words, otherwise it will be obvious that you are being false which, of course, will have an adverse effect.

When you make that extra effort, when you go out of your way to be nice to somebody, for no other reason than to make that person feel good, it's impossible not to feel good yourself. As I've said before, "Life is like a boomerang, in that you always get back what you send out!" If you send out encouragement, smiles, kind words and happiness, that's what you get back. This has a snowball effect, the more you work at it the bigger it becomes. The more you *treat people as you would really like to be treated*, the more they will respond in a likewise manner. Better still, as the "snowball" gathers momentum it becomes stronger and more powerful and therefore, harder to stop! If you make that determined effort for a day, you'll find that it has a knock-on effect. You'll find that the fruits of your labour are so sweet and enjoyable that you'll want to give again the next day and the next. One day will lead to another and before you know it you'll have formed a new behavioural pattern, a new habit. (Remember MADE IT: Make A Determined Effort — Invest the Time.)

Whilst I can't tell you exactly what to say to other people or how you should actually give of yourself, the following suggestions should provide you with a feel for what to do:

1. *Smile to everyone, not a smirk but a genuine warm smile*

A genuine smile always creates folds of skin under your eyes. Go in front of a mirror and try it. It's now been scientifically proven that smiling not only makes the recipient happier but also makes the giver of the smile happier too. In his book, *The Secret Language of Success*, Dr David Lewis, quoting the psychologist Professor R.B. Zajonc of the University of

Michigan, states the reason why smiling makes us feel happier. His explanation goes something like this:

> The face and the brain both obtain blood supply from the same source, the carotid artery. When we frown or smile the facial muscles tighten across the skull, causing the tiny blood vessels to become compressed. This affects the common blood supply in the carotid artery, resulting in slight alterations in the amount of blood supplied to the brain. This, in turn, results in the brain either releasing or surpressing chemical messages to alter our moods.

So there you have it, proof that even if we don't feel like it, if we smile and continue to smile, we will begin to feel happier and that happiness will radiate to others. Thus you could say, a smile increases your face value! The other thing about smiling is that, like laughing, it's contagious. Try smiling to somebody and before long they'll be smiling right back at you. Remember the old saying, "Laugh and the world laughs with you; cry and you cry alone." So then, cheer up someone's day by giving them a smile and at the same time give your face a joy-ride.

The beauty with all this smiling is that it costs nothing. It's been said that a smile is the least expensive and yet the most valuable asset we have. It's also been said that a smile is one little curve that sets a lot of things straight! How very true that is. And whilst we are talking about truisms, let me share with you a final truth about the importance of smiling, in the form of an acronym I once composed and that literally speaks for itself: SMILE — Smiling More Increases Life Expectancy.

2. *Greet everyone cheerfully*

To stand out from the crowd, don't just simply nod your head or raise your eyebrows at someone. Instead, make an effort to greet everyone, and I do mean everyone from the janitor to the chairman, with a real positive and chirpy salutation. From now on, don't just say "morning" or "afternoon" to people, instead take the time to wish that individual, "a good morning to you" or "good afternoon to you." And then be prepared to follow up with a friendly word or two.

3. *Compliment*

   If you look hard enough you will always be able to find something in people to sincerely compliment. Make it a habit to start looking. Brighten up someone else's day and in so doing, you can't help but brighten up your own. (Remember to be sincere!)

4. *Be over-courteous (if there is such a thing).*

   Suffice for me to say that actions often speak louder than words. Here's a poem that I wrote to demonstrate the point:

   Courtesy

   Always be there when you say you will,
   Don't speak or move about when you should be still,
   Open a door, pull out a chair,
   Say please and thank you and show that you care,
   Offer help whenever you can,
   Consider first, your fellow man,
   Ask if they're comfortable, offer a drink,
   Little things mean more than you think,
   Do this and respect their point of view,
   And the best things in life will come to you.

5. *Praise and pat on the back*

   Take the time and make the effort to acknowledge and praise people for a job well done. (To make the recipient feel especially good, dish out your praise in public.) Remember, be sincere and don't overdo it! It's also worth remembering that when you acknowledge and reward good performance you also encourage repeat performance.

6. *Say thank you*

   This, again, is one of those little things that often means so much. Saying thank you, especially to the "little-big people" whom everyone else takes for granted, is worth so much more than those two words could ever reveal. Show people that you are thinking about them, that you appreciate them, that you care, and don't be frightened to do it in public. A public show of gratitude is never forgotten. As an example and without being smug, say something along the lines of, "You know, Sue, I often take what you do for granted but I'd just like to say thank you and well done, I think you do a great job." Then, leave it there and move on. Don't wait around for a response, don't let Sue think there is some ulterior motive behind your words. Another way of saying thanks, and one that's common practice among the winners in life, is to send a thank you note. Taking the trouble to sit down and write a personal word of thanks speaks volumes and shows the recipient that you care. Being bothered enough to make the effort is the mark of the individual who aspires to greatness, the person who really does stand out from the crowd.

7. *Be a nice guy*

Most people see themselves as good, upstanding, law-abiding citizens and that's all very well and proper. However, as my own conscience often reminds me, being a good person doesn't necessarily always make you a nice person!

In today's world of commerce there is an infamous saying, "Nice guys don't win." I'm convinced that this saying was originally devised and spread about by bad guys because the truth is, "Nice guys do win." Certainly some bad guys win as well, but only in the short term. In the long run, bad guys end up behind bars and then worse! That's not what I call winning! On the same theme, there's a bumper sticker, popular with a lot of Porsche owners, that says, "He who dies with the most toys wins." What I'd like to ask them is, wins what?

The real winners in life appreciate and, indeed, have "nice things" but real winners are not so much interested in amassing so-called "toys" and riches which, at best, only provide cosmetic happiness. The real winners in life, those who attain true success and happiness, are "nice guys" who aim to serve rather than be served. The real winners' philosophy is, "It's nice to be important but it's more important to be nice."

8. *Do your good deed for the day*

Now, here's a suggestion for you. Willingly "give" or do *at least* one good deed a day, for the benefit of someone else, for no other reason than to be nice to that person. And remember, it's not what you give that's important; it's the thought that counts. So, give thoughtfully and make a habit of it!

(A good deed is only a genuine good deed when it's undertaken without seeking any form of recompense. After saying that, however, remember that "good deeds, like chickens, always come home to roost!")

9. *Sing, hum, whistle and be a ray of sunshine*

Music, like sunshine, makes people feel happier. It's actually been scientifically proven that sunshine makes people feel happier. I know it does with me. There's nothing quite like feeling the warm, caressing rays of the sun upon your face. And let me ask you this, how many times have your heard a tune being played and then afterwards you find the same tune on your own lips? So then, be a ray of sunshine, sing, hum or whistle a happy tune and let others catch your good cheer!

10. *Don't hold grudges; instead, forgive and forget*

Now, if you really want to stand out from the crowd, here's a challenge for you. Try to be especially nice to someone you don't particularly like or someone who doesn't particularly like you. Why? Well for one thing, harbouring resentment or discord is a major stumbling block to personal enhancement. The plain fact of the matter is, when you are holding grudges you are actually holding yourself back. Put succinctly, forgiveness is a release. Besides which, true forgiveness and humility are both edifying and enlightening.

It's obviously very difficult to dislike someone who is being nice to you. So, go out of your way to be nice to the person you have a disliking for (or dislikes you) and make them like you.

Let me give you an example. Imagine you are walking down a quiet street and on the other side of the road you notice the school bully from years ago. In the intervening years this man has become a nasty, violent criminal, the worst of the worst. He is known as having no respect for anyone or anything and he is feared and despised by all your neighbours and especially by yourself. You quicken your step and put your head down to try and avoid him but Mr Lowlife has spotted you. He scowls, then crosses the road and stops to speak to you. As you nervously stand there, Mr Lowlife's scowl turns into a strained smile and then, rather awkwardly, he says, "You know, as funny as it may seem after all these years, I really respect and admire you... I know that I'm a 'lowlife' and I've done some horrible things in my time... but if I could turn the clock back and have my time over again I'd want to turn out just like you... You know what, you're a really nice guy!" With that Mr Lowlife hesitates for only a second, then he humbly smiles, turns and walks off in the other direction leaving you completely dumbfounded!

Now, how would you feel about your former school bully and the present-day Mr Lowlife? Well, he's not all that bad is he? There must be a streak or two of goodness in him. And deep down, I'll bet he's really got a heart of gold. It's just that he's had a tough upbringing, he's had a rough time and been through a lot and it's difficult for him to show his true self. And the next time one of your neighbours has something derogative to say about Mr Lowlife, how are you going to react? I think it's a pretty fair assumption to say that you will fight his corner, you will stick up for him and defend him. Why? Because Mr Lowlife likes you, he as much as told you so. And it's very difficult to dislike someone who likes you.

So then, if you are holding any grudges, if you dislike someone or their behaviour towards you — then make the first move, say something to make amends and, as the saying goes, "don't delay, do it today". Edwin Louis Cole wrote, "There are times when silence is golden, other times it is just plain yellow." Don't be yellow! Make the first move. Be courageous. Be bold. You can never be sure of what the other person's response will be but if the forgiveness is not mutual, let it be their problem and not yours. If you want to stand out from the crowd, if you really do aspire to greatness then you must be willing to take action. Life is too short to hold grudges, so deal with yours straight away and remember one last thing, "no one ever choked swallowing their pride!"

As we are looking at this principle of *"treating people how you would really like to be treated"* and showing how a person inadvertently benefits from serving others, let's now look at a few more traits of a winner, the person who stands out from the crowd. Now I'm not, for one moment, trying to suggest that you have to adopt the following behaviours in order to find true success and happiness in life, but one thing I am certain of, doing so will only benefit your cause. As I've said before, to stand out from the crowd is to be different, to be bothered, to make a difference however large or small and to, ultimately, feel good about the role you play.

The best way to demonstrate some of these characteristic behaviours or attributes is by way of example. On the whole, we live in a society where negativity reigns, so let's take a look at how the winners in life react to some everyday occurrences in our negative society.

For example, we live in a negative society where people respond to an enquiry after their health with the affirmation, "I'm not so bad." It's almost as though they are expecting to be bad or even worse! So, from now on, when people ask how you are, be different. Be positive. If you're well, say, "I'm feeling great and I'm glad to be alive." On the other hand, if you're sick, say, "I'm not so good but I'm improving all the time."

We live in a negative society where weather forecasters talk about the chances of rain. People complain when it's raining because it's too wet. They complain when it's cold and say that it's freezing. They complain when it's cloudy and wish for sunshine. And they complain when the sun's shining because it's too hot. (There really is no pleasing some people!) The truth is, every day is a wonderful day, regardless of the weather. (Those people who don't agree, should try missing a day... then they'd see just how wonderful each one really is!) I might be an optimist but at the same time, I'm also a pragmatist and so I'm the first to accept that life is not always a bed of roses. Therefore, what I'm alluding to here, is not so much that you don't ever have an "off day" but that life itself or every day doesn't become an "off day".

Again, we live in a negative society where so many people live for the weekend. These people simply wish their lives away. At the beginning of the week they suffer from the Monday morning blues as they realise they have a full week ahead of them. However, by the close of business on Wednesdays, they cheer up a little as they point out to everyone else that there are only two days left to go! They spend all week waiting for the weekend and all weekend dreading the forthcoming week. Sad, isn't it?

Yes, unfortunately, there's no question about it, we do live in a negative society. But you, as an individual, can do something about it. You can choose to be different, you can choose to stand out from the crowd, to dispose of negative attitudes and behaviour and to do your little bit to make this world a better place in which to live. At the end of the day it is simply a matter of choice. Take, for example, some of the following choices which in themselves don't add up to much, but on the whole, make a world of difference to the individual who makes them! These examples once again characterise the positive attributes of a winner or the person who aspires to be a winner.

♦ The winners in life are the kind of people who, when walking in the countryside or at the seaside, will pick up other people's litter. Not because they want to be seen as "do-gooders" nor to draw attention to themselves, but simply because they care. They're the people who appreciate God's creation, so much so that they hate to see it spoiled. A winner knows that it's impossible to pick up every piece of litter and that often their efforts are futile, but the person who stands out from the crowd knows, it's not the quantity of effort that makes the difference, so much as the attitude involved in the act!

♦ The winners in life are the kind of people who recycle and do their bit to protect the environment. In today's age of convenience foods, excess packaging, junk mail and free local newspapers, etc., the winning attitude is one of "waste not want not". Certainly, being "green conscious" and recycling is time-consuming and an inconvenience at the best of times, but again the overall attitude is one of caring. Caring enough about our world and our future generations to do something about it. The winner's philosophy is to treat the earth and our environment, not as though it were given to us by our parents but as though it were lent to us by our children.

♦ The winners in life are the courteous kind of people who give way to other motorists just for the fun of it. Now and again, everyone gets stuck in rush hour traffic or else they find themselves behind a Sunday driver (the ones who always wear a hat and travel everywhere at 30 kph). There again, everyone has experienced traffic jams and the drivers who constantly change lanes in order to try and gain a few extra metres. In these and similar situations there is often nothing we can do about it, or is there? Well, we may not be able to anything to change the actual situation but we can change our attitude towards the situation. Being patient, courteous and considerate of other drivers is, at the end of the day, simply a choice. Besides which, you get a real deep-down feeling of satisfaction when you give way to a fellow driver, when you smile warmly and wave them through. Try it! At the end of the day, there are road ragers and there are road rangers! Once again, it's all just a matter of choice.

♦ The winners in life are the kind of people who, on a day off, still make the effort to make themselves presentable. For example, a woman will make-up her face and hair and a man will still shave, etc. Why? Because they care about their appearance, not just to the outside world (the work-place and business colleagues, etc.) but also to the inside world, their family and the people they care for. A winner doesn't just put on a show from 9 till 5, Monday to Friday. A winner has that deep-down conviction which causes them to live each day of their lives with the same values. (Please understand that I'm not saying a moustache, beard or even deliberate designer stubble is inappropriate. What I am saying is that a winner doesn't "slob out" on a day off because a winner's attitudes are not affected by the days of the week.)

♦ The winners in life are the kind of people who feed the birds, especially in winter. As inconsequential as this may seem when we're talking about success, this is one of those little things that, again, makes such a big difference. It's the caring or being bothered enough to act, it's the consideration of other things for the overall good, things that others may feel are inconsequential. That's the difference that makes the winners in life stand out from the crowds.

Here's a final illustration of a winner, someone who is committed to making a difference. It's a story about a man taking a stroll along a beach. As he was walking along the man noticed someone in the distance, who kept bending down to pick something up and then, almost delicately, throwing it into the ocean.

As he came closer the man saw thousands of starfish washed up by the high tide and now left stranded and dying on the beach. He observed a young man picking up the starfish and one by one tossing them gently back into the water. After watching this seemingly futile effort, the observer said, "Young man, I'm afraid you're wasting your time. There are literally thousands of starfish washed up on this beach and, for that matter, probably on every beach along this coastline. It would be impossible for you to save them all or even to make the slightest difference." The young man smiled but there was a determined look in his eye as he bent down to pick up another starfish. Tossing it gently back into the ocean he turned to the older man and replied, "It made a difference to that one."

Let me finish off by asking you again, will you commit yourself to making a difference? Will you be known as one who stands out from the crowds? I trust your answer will be a resounding YES.

Yours cordially,

Uncle Bob

CHAPTER SIXTEEN

Look After Yourself

"If a man doesn't take care of No.1, he will soon have 0 to take care of." (Charles Dickens.)

Dear Go-getter,

IN THIS LETTER, by looking after yourself, I'm not talking about being selfish or putting your own interests before those of others. Rather, looking after number one, to borrow the words of Charles Dickens, pertains to looking after the most precious and priceless piece of equipment needed to achieve, sustain and more importantly, enjoy, success — namely, YOU!

The human body, in fact life itself, really is priceless. Think about it, what man on his deathbed wouldn't give away everything he owned for a few more breaths of life! When the US oil tycoon and multi-millionaire J. Paul Getty died in 1976, a reporter asked, "How much money did Mr Getty leave behind?" The answer, of course, is all of it! J. Paul Getty left all his money behind. He did, however, enjoy life for some 86 years before doing so! The point I'm trying to make is this: Having all the riches in the world is worthless if you don't have the health or the time to enjoy them. And yet the tragic truth is that too many people take their bodies and their health for granted. So much so, that they literally and constantly abuse their most valuable possession. Too much stress, too much work, too much over-indulgence, lack of exercise, lack of good diet, lack of rest and recuperation and so on. The list is often overwhelming and depressing but the good news is, it needn't be. The fact is, it's never too late to make a fresh start. Never!

If you're not already serious about keeping yourself in good shape physically, then you'll reply to what I'm about to say with either the "fight" or "flight" response. Either you'll determine to fight and do something about it or alternatively, you'll flee from the truth and put off doing anything about it until some later date. I hope you will choose the first response!

Most people realise, to the point of feeling guilty, that they really should make an effort to keep fit, to look after their physical well-being, and yet they end up doing little or nothing about it. Instead, they satisfy their guilty consciences by resolving to do something about it... soon. The diet that's going to start next week, the new exercise programme to begin... whenever! And the saddest reason of all, is the extra time they'll have to do all these things just as soon as they finish that important project at work or just as soon as they become less busy! At the time these "reasons" are voiced they are often not so much excuses but genuine intentions to actually do something about the situation. And because the intentions are genuine (at the time), the conscience is then appeased and so fades into the background, out of sight out of mind as it were. However, as the genuine intentions are put to one side for later, they also begin to lose their power and they too fade away into the background. The inevitable conclusion is that, once again, no action is taken.

The sad reality is that most people are only concerned enough to actually do something about getting into shape or looking after their health, when they haven't got it anymore or there's a threat of losing it. The plain fact is, making the commitment to look after yourself physically, as well as mentally and spiritually, takes an enormous amount of discipline which is always uncomfortable, for a while at least. A change of lifestyle or behaviour means forcing yourself out of your comfort zone time and time again, until your new behaviour pattern becomes a part of you.

Let me give you a very simple example to demonstrate this point. Please put this letter down in front of you so that you can still read it and then fold your arms. Note which arm (the right or the left) you placed on top of the other. Let's call this position your comfort zone. Now, what I want you to do is fold your arms the other way around so that the opposite arm is now on top. Notice how awkward and uncomfortable this feels. I'm sure you will agree that it requires an effort to sustain this new position, because what you really want to do is return to your original position, your comfort zone, don't you? My point is this: If you were to discipline yourself to stick with it, if every time you crossed your arms you made a deliberate effort to adopt this new position, then before long this new position would become more comfortable to you. Like I said, changing your lifestyle or behaviour patterns means forcing yourself out of your comfort zone, time and time again, until your new behaviour becomes a part of you.

When it comes down to implementing a regular exercise programme you can have the best intentions in the world but, of course, to win you have to first of all begin. As I've said before, the hardest part of doing anything is getting started. In fact, getting started is actually half the battle. The other half comes down to that old familiar story of persistence or what's known in the fitness world as repetition! The problem with a lot of people is that even when they do start and begin a programme of self-improvement, all too often many of them quit and end up returning to their old ways. This often happens because people become disillusioned when they don't see any immediate results. Feeling disheartened they take their eyes off the goal and then, sadly, it always seems pointless to continue any further so they throw in the towel and quit. These individuals are often so near and yet so far away. They fail to wholly understand that persistence always conquers resistance, eventually. Listen again to these wise words from Thomas Edison, "Many of life's failures are people who did not realise how close they were to success when they gave up."

Once again we're back on to that old subject of persistence. What it really comes down to is this: The winners in life persist until they succeed, then continue to persist and continue to succeed. Understand then, that it's not a one-time massive effort that makes the major difference but an ongoing persistent effort. Being a one-day wonder or a weekend warrior when it comes to physically looking after yourself, whilst obviously better than nothing is still inadequate. It is regular exercise — repetition — that makes the difference.

Regular exercise increases your stamina and makes you sharper and more alert mentally. No doubt, you'll be familiar with the saying, "A healthy body leads to a healthy mind". Regular exercise makes you healthier and less prone to common ailments such as colds or influenza as well as major illnesses such as diabetes or heart conditions. Regular exercise makes you feel good about yourself, it increases your self-esteem because it makes you feel fit and alive which helps to keep you feeling young. Regular exercise increases your metabolism, which burns up the extra calories and helps to keep your weight under control. Most important of all, regular exercise increases your chances of a longer, healthier life which means you'll have more time to enjoy your blessings and booty with your loved ones.

So then, appreciate that the greatest asset we all have, the finest tool we possess, the most powerful instrument in the whole world, incorporating an onboard computer with capabilities far beyond our comprehension, indeed, the most precious thing in existence, is life, your life, YOU! Now let me ask you this; doesn't it make sense to look after you physically, as well as mentally and spiritually? Doesn't it make sense to maintain you in good working order? Doesn't it make sense to persist and continue to do so?

Imagine for a moment, a taxi driver not maintaining his vehicle (his most precious asset), but instead running into the ground! For a time, when the taxi is new and reliable, the driver makes a good living and he's comfortable. He has the best intentions in the world and he plans to service his vehicle regularly. He agrees with the phrase, "prevention is better than cure" and knows that it makes a lot of sense to look after the asset he depends most upon to earn his living. But, all the same, there seems to be no urgency to do anything about it at this precise moment, so it doesn't matter putting it off, for a little while at least. Besides which, the taxi is still young and running perfectly well so the driver doesn't anticipate there will be any problems! However, that's not to say that he doesn't still plan to service his vehicle. In fact, he intends to do so very soon. But for now his philosophy is more along the lines of, "if it ain't broke don't fix it." Anyway, there seems very little point in spending good money unnecessarily. The taxi driver decides that he will begin servicing his vehicle straight after the Christmas and New Year holidays, when business slackens off a bit. Now that he has actually made a plan (a genuine plan I might add), he starts to feel better and so he allows himself to fall back into the comfort zone.

Meanwhile, business is good and although the taxi (which is constant use) is now in need of a few very minor repairs and a couple of adjustments here and there, it's nothing that can't wait for a week or two. This continues but the driver still genuinely intends to put his vehicle in for a thorough service as soon as he can find the time. It's just that at the moment it seems such a pity to take the taxi off the road while there are such rich pickings to be had. In any event, it's good business sense to make hay while the sun shines!

Alas, the months pass by and the taxi driver is either too busy and can't afford the time or else he's too quiet, takings are down and he can't afford the money or the time off work. Then there was that extra expense at home, then the extra cash needed for holidays, then the computer for his eldest son and then the problems with the new competition in the area, threatening to poach his accounts. Still, the taxi was a young vehicle, no longer new perhaps, but there was still plenty of life left in the old girl yet! And she definitely was going to get a major overhaul and refurbishment just as soon as... BANG! Time ran out for the poor old taxi driver. The taxi had a serious breakdown, which meant it being off the road for several weeks, possibly even months. The mechanics didn't hold out much hope and said that, although the body work looked okay, really the taxi needed a new engine because the old one had simply been run into the ground. Poor Mr Taxi Driver, he ended up losing everything that he'd spent his life working for!

Now, let me ask you again, doesn't it make sense to look after yourself? Doesn't it make sense to maintain yourself in good working order? Doesn't it make sense to persist and continue to do so? If you're not already committed to looking after yourself, I want to encourage you to start right away, today if possible. All too often I hear people say that they can't afford the time but those people, in particular, are the ones who can't afford not to find the time. The fact is, if something is important enough to us, then we'll find the time for it! I shall cover the subject of managing time in my next letter but for now, suffice for me to say that we must plan our time and then time our plan. (Then stick to it come what may!)

Now, I'm not suggesting that you become some sort of fitness fanatic but a minimum exercise programme should be at least 20+ minutes, three times a week and strenuous enough to ensure that you build up a sweat. Obviously, if you have any doubts about exercising you should seek medical advice first. The rule here is, don't not do it, just don't over do it!

As I've said before, keeping in shape and being physically fit is important to me and so I personally try to go jogging at least three times a week. I also have a bicycle which I use as often as I can and (at the time of writing) I also try to fit in a game of squash once a week. Now finding the time for this exercise is sometimes very difficult but because it's important to me, I make it a matter of priority. You should do the same and make it a priority in your own life.

Our diet, watching our weight or looking after our figure is something else that everyone struggles with from time to time, some more than others, of course. Here again, it's discipline that makes the difference. The fact is, as Zig Ziglar puts it, we have chosen to be the weight that we are because we have never eaten anything unintentionally or by accident. Enjoying a well-balanced diet doesn't mean that we have to abstain from the odd treat or the occasional so called "junk" food, but it is good to remember that we eat to live not live to eat. The American statesman, scientist and author Benjamin Franklin, who helped draw up the Declaration of Independence, also had some wise words to say about our diet. Let me leave you with the following advice taken from his book, *Poor Richard's Almanack*. "Three good meals a day is bad living: To lengthen thy life lessen thy meals."

Well that's about all for now. Until next time, look after yourself and remember — don't delay, start today.

Yours fittingly,

Uncle Bob

CHAPTER SEVENTEEN

Finding the Time

'To waste your time is to waste your life, but to master your time is to master your life.' (Anon.)

Dear Go-getter,

OVER RECENT YEARS much has been said and written about the art of time management, and yet, this is not a new subject. In fact, some 2,300 years ago, the Greek philosopher Aristotle said, "Like all things time must be managed." In this letter I hope to show you how to do just that.

I have no intention, however, of getting involved in a long drawn-out thesis or producing countless theories and suggestions about spending a certain amount of time for this and that. Let it be enough for me to say that there can often be so many demands on our time that frequently there will not be enough time in a day to literally do everything. The only solution to this problem, of finding the time, is to prioritise. And this, at the end of the day, is nothing more than good old common sense.

Time management is not at all complicated. In fact, it can be very simply summarised into these two words: PRIORITISE and DISCIPLINE. If we prioritise the things we have to do and we discipline ourselves to stick to our agenda, then we manage our time effectively and are always at our most productive. In other words, if we plan our time and time our plan we will get a lot more things done and done more effectively. That's not to say that we won't occasionally get bogged down in work or that we will always be able to find the time to do the things we want to do. As I've already said, there are often so many demands on our time that there are not enough hours in the day to literally do everything. We must, therefore, prioritise and choose how we spend our time.

For example, people frequently say, "I really need to spend more time with my family but I'm just so busy" or "I know I should exercise more but with my schedule I just can't find the time" or "I would love to paint, write a book, take cookery classes or whatever, but it's just finding the time!" What these people are really saying is that whatever it is they would like to do or, indeed, *know* that they should do, is just not important enough for them to actually find the time to do. (At least, not at the present.)

Allow me to expand a little further. Let's say that you want to spend more time with your family or get into shape or learn a new language or study for an exam or whatever it is you've been telling yourself for ages that you really should find the time to do. Now here's a suggestion. Why not just set aside an hour every day, say for the next 28 days, so that you can do whatever it is that you can never seem to find the time to do? To this suggestion most people would simply say, "An hour a day for 28 days? Impossible!"

Now let me rephrase the above example. Supposing I said, if you spend an hour a day for 28 days, just doing the thing that you really want to do anyway, I'll give you $10,000 cash! All of a sudden, this has thrown a new perspective on things. The task now takes on a new importance and no matter what demands you have on your time, you'll find the extra hour each day, right? This simply goes to illustrate my earlier point that when people say the can't find the time, what they're actually saying, is that whatever it is, it's not really important enough to them, (at that moment) to actually find the time to do it.

It's the same when a person is invited out to lunch but declines, saying that they are just too busy, or when a father can't find the time to come and watch his child in the school play. What is really being said in these situations is, "I'm sorry but right now, it's just not important enough for me to give it my time!" In other words the person prioritises their time, albeit sometimes unwittingly! The fact is, we all prioritise our time, albeit sometimes unwittingly. But whether or not we always make the right priorities is another question!

Let me put it this way: Each day is a valuable and very important day because no matter how you choose to spend it, you've agreed to trade a day of your life for it. Given the choice, would you rather spend a day of your life being busy with things that won't matter at all in just a little while, or would you rather spend it doing something meaningful and worthwhile? Well, guess what? You have that choice, indeed you make that very choice every day of your life. So you see, when we prioritise our time we should always make sure that we give the highest priority to that with is the most beneficial, the most worthwhile.

As author and public speaker Rob Parsons often says, "Nobody on their death bed ever said, 'I wish I'd spent more time at the office!' " The fact is, no one will ever remember how much time you spent at work, except maybe your family and other loved ones you leave behind. Benjamin Franklin very profoundly wrote, "Lost time is never found." That is so true! There is no such thing as recapturing the moment. When the moment is passed, it is passed and gone forever. I want to encourage you to PRIORITISE now, before it's too late, especially when it comes to spending time with your loved ones! And please don't fall into the trap of saying that it's the quality and not the quantity of time that counts. That saying is a load of old baloney, probably made up by an overworked executive to ease his guilty conscience. The fact is, you can only enjoy quality time if you put in quantity time! Think about it.

And as I'm talking about prioritising your time, here's something else to think about, in the form of a verse titled "Take Time":

> *Take time to THINK... it is the source of power.*
> *Take time to PLAY... it is the secret of perpetual youth.*
> *Take time to READ... it is the fountain of wisdom.*
> *Take time to PRAY... it is the greatest power on earth.*

Take time to LOVE and BE LOVED... it is a God-given
    privilege.
Take time to BE FRIENDLY... it is the road to happiness.
Take time to LAUGH... it is the music of the soul.
Take time to GIVE... it is too short a day to be selfish.
Take time to WORK... it is the price of success.
Take time to DO CHARITY... it is the key to heaven.

Now let's move on and talk for a moment about DISCIPLINE. We do indeed trade a day of our life for every 24 hours, but how we actually spend that time is left for each of us to decide, for most part at least. As I have suggested once before, imagine what results could be achieved by disciplining yourself and choosing to spend, say, just 1 per cent of your time each day in study or learning a new skill.

Each day or 24 hours consists of 1,440 minutes, so 1 per cent of each day is equivalent to only 14.4 minutes. Now everybody alive can find an extra 14.4 minutes a day if they want to do! When you add it up, spending 1 per cent of your time each day in study (rounded up, that's 15 minutes a day) adds up to over 91 hours of additional learning over the course of a year. If you will do this, if you will discipline yourself to spend just 1 per cent of your time each day on some form of self-improvement programme, then it won't take long before you start to see some amazing results. Again, anybody can find that amount of time if they really want to — it's just a question of discipline.

I thought it would be useful to share some of the ways that I try to make better and more effective use of my own time. The following techniques are simple procedures that I've adopted and adapted into my own life. I encourage you to do the same.

1. *Relaxation*

We achieve so much more with our time when we are focused; when we are in the right frame of mind, so to speak. The following technique is one that has been practised by some of the greatest minds throughout history and one that is still commonly practised by many successful people today. Just as exercising our bodies ultimately gives us more energy, so relaxation gives us more mental ability and enables us to re-focus our efforts with renewed concentration. With regular daily practice complete relaxation can be achieved in a matter of a few minutes but, just like a recharged battery, the benefits are then apparent for many hours to come.

Here's what to do. Sometime during the course of your day take five to ten minutes to relax, unwind and recharge those mental batteries. If you're in the car, recline the seat. If you're in the office, shut the door, hold your calls, put your feet up or preferably, lie down. Close your eyes and take one or two deep breaths. Then slowly count backwards from ten down to zero, whilst regulating your breathing into short shallow breaths and relaxing. Now concentrate on letting go of the tension from every part of your body. Feel each muscle and limb become heavy as you focus your mind on releasing the tension in each part of your body. Start with your feet. Give the mental command to relax and feel them become limp and heavy as your muscles loosen. Then move up your body slowly, giving the mental command each time. Your calves... relax... your knees... relax... your thighs... relax... your buttocks... relax. Next feel your stomach, shoulders, arms, hands. Then your neck and head including your face and scalp, all the time consciously letting go.

After a couple of minutes of this, once you are fully relaxed, condition your mind using positive self-talk, auto-suggestions and affirmations spoken in silence, e.g. — "I am now completely relaxed. My energy and enthusiasm levels are being recharged. In a moment or two I shall become completely awake again and then I will feel refreshed and replenished. I will have renewed strength, my ability will increase and I will succeed in the task ahead of me." Finally, after two, three or four minutes of this, when you're completely peaceful, then reverse the counting process. This time slowly count from one to ten, telling yourself that on the count of ten you will become completely awake, full of energy and ready to start over. It might interest you to know that I frequently use this technique when I'm writing and need renewed energy or fresh inspiration.

2. *Plan for tomorrow at the end of today*

Nowadays, there are many trainers and writers who go to great lengths to produce plans, theories and suggestions on how to save time or how we can create more time or make better use of our time, etc. Whilst many of these have very fine-sounding arguments, the fact of the matter is that for many successful people the only actual time-planning exercise they do, is to create a "things to do" list at the end of each day.

Just before you shut up shop and head off for home, sit down quietly and spend a few minutes planning for tomorrow. Write down on a piece of paper a list of all the things you need to do and then run through the list and number each entry in order of priority. Tomorrow's plan of action is now mapped out in front of you. Tomorrow you start at number 1, the most important item, and work your way through the list, crossing off as you go. Any item that doesn't get crossed off you simply put onto the next day's list, although you might want to give it a higher priority. Simple but very, very effective!

There are two important reasons why you should make your "things to do" list at the end of each day. Firstly, creating a list relieves your mind from the pressure of having to remember everything. This helps you to switch off and allows you to go home in the right frame of mind to recharge your batteries and spend time with the people you care about. And secondly, at the end of the day is when your energy level is at its lowest. What better time to relax quietly and prepare tomorrow's plan of action. In a nutshell, it makes a lot more sense to concentrate on your "things to do" list at the end of your day, then you can concentrate on actually doing the things that need to be done when you're fresh and raring to go, in the morning.

3. *Delegate*

It's been said that the art of good management is to do yourself out of a job! In other words: delegate. First and foremost then, the art of good management is to train your staff or employees so that they are competent enough for you to delegate work to them. The best time management principle there is, is this one: Concentrate at all times on doing whatever is the most productive. This, of course, often means that certain work must be delegated. This has a two-fold effect. It frees you up so that you can do other things and at the same time it also brings on or helps to develop your subordinates. At this point I'd like to make it clear that delegate doesn't mean relegate. In other words, I am not condoning that you hold on to work that you enjoy doing and pass everything else on to someone else. That would hardly be good and effective management of other people!

Only an insecure manager with a low self-esteem refuses to delegate his work. Such a person tries to become a kind of one-man workforce, a would-be hero; he needs to feel indispensable and so jealously guards his own duties. The really unfortunate thing though, is that in not delegating his work, the "indispensable" man rarely has any time for anything else other than work. Ironically, however, there is in actual fact no such thing as an indispensable man, as the following poem (author anonymous) clearly demonstrates.

The Indispensable Man

Sometime, when you're feeling important,
Sometime, when your ego's in bloom,
Sometime, when you take it for granted,
You're the best informed man in the room.

Take a bucket and fill it with water,
Put your hand in it up to the wrist,
Pull it out and the hole that remains there,
Is the measure of how you'll be missed.

You may splash all you please as you enter,
You may stir up the waters galore,
But stop and you'll see in a moment,
That it looks just the same as before.

The moral of this little story,
Is do just the best you can,

'Cause you'll find that in spite of vain glory,
There is no indispensable man.

In conclusion then, remember to delegate whenever you can and make better use of the time you save by doing so.

4. *Stand up for power meetings*

This is one of my favourites for saving time and keeping business meetings focused and on track. Instead of sitting comfortably around the boardroom table for a leisurely and time-consuming meeting, remove the chairs and hold the meeting standing up. You'll find that meetings come very much straight down to business. Short and sweet, but also very effective!

5. *Make optimum use of the waste paper basket*

Don't waste any of your time reading triviality or useless, unnecessary information, instead bin it! Don't clutter up your in-tray, desk drawers or your mind with hoards of "stuff" that you intend to look through at a later date. If it's not important don't waste your time on it, simply put it in the waste paper basket, or better still, think green and think, recycle paper centre!

Another thing, get in to the habit of handling paperwork once and once only, as soon as you get it. Remember again, "Never put off till tomorrow what you can do today." When it comes to paperwork either action it, bin it or recycle it but whatever you do, do it now and get it out of the way.

On my desk in my office I have an ornamental paperweight in the form of a decorative wooden ball with the letters "TUIT" printed on top of it. In actual fact, to give it its full name, the item is known as "A Round Tuit". The "Round Tuit" symbolises work that has been put off or put to one side until later, until I get around to it *(A Round Tuit)*. I must admit that I don't often use the "Round Tuit" as a paperweight for work that I've not yet gotten around to but nevertheless, it remains on my desk as a stark reminder to deal with my paperwork straight away.

6. *Work smarter not harder*

For fear of not quoting the obvious, here's a little classic that allows you to do two things in half the amount of time, i.e. do two things at once! For example, I use a Walkman whilst taking exercise which allows me to train mentally and physically at the same time. Likewise, when travelling I'll listen to an audio cassette or CD, or I'll read to learn or brush up on my skills. Often I'll combine business and food into a business lunch and then of course, like most other businesspeople, I try to make optimum use of today's technology and time-saving devices such as the lap-top computer, email, mobile telephone and Dictaphone, etc.

7. *Switch off the TV*

For my thinking, one of the most effective time-saving devices in the world is a simple little switch on everyone's TV set with the words ON/OFF printed beside it. When the television set is switched on it becomes addictive and some people will, quite literally, watch anything. Even when there is nothing on the TV that they really want to watch, a lot of folk, rather than switch it off, will simply use the remote control to flick from channel to channel. In the end they sit there almost comatosed, watching any old rubbish for 20 minutes or so, until something a little better (or worse) begins on another channel. Now I'm not suggesting, for one moment, there is anything wrong with slouching in front of the TV every once in a while, just so long as it doesn't become a nightly habit.

If, by any chance, I've just hit a nerve then here's a suggestion for you that, with DISCIPLINE, can literally save you many extra hours each week, hours of precious time that you can then put to much better use. At the beginning of the week take the TV guide and browse through it, making a note of the programmes for the coming week that you want to watch. Then discipline yourself to only watch the TV at those specific times. Alternatively, you can always record the programmes and then watch them later, maybe even all in one sitting!

In summary, let me say it again, there will always be many demands on our time but managing our time effectively isn't really difficult or complicated. It all comes down to those two key words, PRIORITY and DISCIPLINE. I believe this is what Francis Bacon was alluding to when he wrote, "To choose time is to save time!" I trust you will choose yours wisely.

Yours cordially,

Uncle Bob

CHAPTER EIGHTEEN

Family Matters

"The family that plays together stays together." (Motto found on box of the Trivial Pursuit board game.)

Dear Go-getter,

I SET OUT to share with you some of my insights for winning and achieving results in this game of life and we have now covered most of the important issues. Now, finally, I have one last subject that I want to include: family.

Let me start by stating a fact. True success, fulfilment and lasting happiness is only ever possible when we have others to share it with. Our family are the ones who make all our efforts and everything else seem worthwhile. It's our family which give us real purpose and meaning in life and this, especially, pertains to our spouse. Of course, our children are very important but sooner or later they will leave home to begin their own family, and so continue the process of procreation, as indeed they are meant to do. But for a husband and wife it's different. They are meant to be life-long companions, lovers and friends who are joined together to become "as one flesh". Now, of course, I'm writing this piece from a man's point of view but the fact remains that when it comes down to achieving true success (not material wealth) and lasting happiness, your wife (husband) is the most important person in the world.

Unfortunately, however, some men don't realise this and all too often they take their families and especially their wife for granted. (Nowadays, as more and more women succeed in the workplace, the same can also be said about wives. However, being a man, I shall continue from a man's perspective.) In their quest to get on in life and achieve wealth and status, many men become overly obsessed with the pursuit of riches and power — so much so, that they often lose sight of the fact that they are distancing themselves from their loved ones.

When work life becomes more important and continually takes a higher priority than family life, a man will never find true success, happiness or fulfilment. Obviously, there are times when our work is so important that it must take priority. I do not dispute that. But the point I am trying to make here is that our work is not so important that it should always take priority. Remember Rob Parsons' poignant phrase, "Nobody on their death bed ever said 'I wish I'd spent more time at the office!' "

The plain truth is that our wife and family are far more important than the pursuit of riches, power and status but unfortunately, a lot of men don't wholly realise this until it's too late. And yet the fact is, a man cannot achieve true success and happiness by himself, simply because he needs other people. As John Donne wrote, "No man is an island". Let me expand on this a little further with the following example.

On 17 December 1903, the Wright brothers, Orville and Wilbur, secured a place in the history books by becoming the very first men to fly. This event was a giant step for aviation and one that pointed others in the right direction. From then on, the human quest to fly moved forward at a rapid pace. In fact, in the same generation as mankind's first ever flight, men also flew in space for the very first time. And then, only a few years later, men flew to the moon, landed and walked on the surface of another planet. It was 3.56 a.m. (British summer time) on 21 July 1969 when the American astronaut, Neil Armstrong, took his first step on the moon. As his feet touched the ground he spoke the now famous words, "That's one small step for man, one giant leap for mankind."

Now, although Neil Armstrong is the name that went down in the history books, although he is the one who received the acclaim and the one who will be remembered for all time, there were also many others behind the scenes who made that first step possible. Once you acknowledge this fact, you begin to realise that to attain and, more importantly, maintain success you need the help and support of others. And that's what I want to talk about here, the importance of the other people in your life; but especially so, your wife.

It's true that many people achieve wealth, power and status by their own efforts. Such people are often referred to as self-made! But for all their achievements, these self-made "success" stories can often be heard to say, "It's lonely at the top." The reason for this is that true success is always coupled with happiness and the only way it's possible to attain and maintain this kind of success, is with the help and support of others. And the most important other person, once again, the one who is capable of contributing the most towards this true success is, without doubt, your spouse. I once read the following witticism that sums this up beautifully. "Behind every successful man there's a good woman." Understanding this is a giant step in the right direction!

The truth is, when you look at any truly successful person you'll find that their success always begins at home. You see a man's wife can either be his best ally or his worst enemy and the reality is, that choice is usually made by the husband! If a man shares with his wife and they make plans together, if he communicates with her and spends time with her and shows affection to her, she will be his best ally. But, on the other hand, if he works every hour that God sends, if he doesn't communicate or share, if he neglects the physical and emotional needs of his family, then his wife can and often does become his worst enemy!

At the end of the day we strive to succeed so that we can enjoy the benefits of our success with the people that we love. Indeed, success means nothing at all if you have no one to share it with! Yet all too often, the trap for many men is to become so engrossed in their work that they neglect the ones they're really working for. All too often, the man ambitious for success and riches becomes oblivious to the fact that in working flat-out for the good of his family, he is in actual fact doing the opposite and working flat-out to destroy his family. Unfortunately, it is not uncommon to hear an indignant, sad and sometimes wealthy man complaining that his wife has left him, and after he has struggled for so many years to provide her with such a good lifestyle! In his continuous quest for betterment, he has put his love for wealth and power before the love of his wife and family. He has become selfish with his time and unintentionally neglected the people he cares most for. But ironically, he doesn't realise this until it's too late. He's been kidding himself for years that quieter times would come and that all his hard work really was for the good of his family. Sadly though, the only thing his wife and children ever really wanted from the "busy-ness man" was his time, the one thing that all the wealth, power and status in the world can't buy!

Now, I am not suggesting that people shouldn't work hard. Quite the opposite in fact. Often, it is very necessary to work hard and long hours in order to both provide for the family and also achieve career success, as indeed I have had to do myself. Sometimes sacrifices have to be made. I know that all too well, but the emphasis here is *sometimes*, not constantly, all the time! The Bible states, "A man reaps what he sows." (Galations 6:7) This, of course, is true in all areas of life but especially so in marriage.

I am also not suggesting there is anything wrong with wanting to be wealthy. There is nothing at all wrong with wanting to be rich, just as long as making money doesn't become your obsession or your god. Lady Margaret Thatcher once said, "No one would remember the Good Samaritan if he'd only had good intentions. He had money as well." Money is intrinsically good and there is absolutely nothing wrong with having lots of it! It's often been said that money is evil but that's not true, rather it's the love of money or the chasing after money wherein lies the evil. Again, the Bible has many important things to say on this subject of money. The following quotes are a few examples:

♦ "Keep your lives free from the love of money." (Hebrews 13:5)

♦ "The love of money is the root of all kinds of evil."
(1 Timothy 6:9)

♦ "Whoever loves money never has money enough; whoever loves wealth is never satisfied with his income."
(Ecclesiastes 5:10)

♦ "Do not wear yourself out to get rich; have the wisdom to show restraint. (Proverbs 23:4)

If your life is simply money, money, money, if it's money that makes your world go around, then you'll never have enough of it and furthermore, you will never find real happiness. NEVER. I personally know many rich men, several of them multi-millionaires, but for the most part, even with all their business success and wealth, very few of them are genuinely happy or contented. However, there are some wealthy individuals I know, who most definitely are happy and successful. For these individuals there seem to be two things that set them apart from the rest. Firstly, making money is not their overall priority. Certainly it's important but it's not the most important! An old associate of mine, Stewart, used to say, "Sometimes life is more important than making money." That about sums it up! Secondly, the other thing that sets these individuals apart, is that they invest time with their family and in every case they are happily married.

Let's look at these two issues a little deeper. First of all, money. This is what I mean by putting money into the right perspective:

♦ Money can buy you a house but it can't buy you a home.

♦ Money can buy you a bed but it can't buy you sleep.

♦ Money can buy you companionship but it can't buy you friendship.

- Money can buy you medicine but it can't buy you good health.

- Money can buy you a holiday but it can't buy you rest.

- Money can buy you investments but it can't buy you peace of mind.

- Money can buy you a pension but it can't buy you a happy retirement.

- Money can buy you food but it can't buy you an appetite.

- Money can buy you entertainment but it can't buy you happiness.

- Money can buy you lots of things but it can't buy you love or self worth.

So you see, money is intrinsically good. You can buy and do a lot of good things with it, but the pursuit of money is not and must not be everything. It is a means, not an end. In the final analysis, it's okay to have money and possess things as long as money and things don't possess you. In both business and family life the key word to true success is BALANCE. Balance means: it's good to be able to afford the things money can buy but only if it doesn't costs us the things that money can't buy! This leads us onto the second issue, marriage.

To achieve balance it's necessary to invest time with your wife and family. Marriage is a partnership and like any partnership, the main ingredient for a happy and fulfilling relationship is communication, coupled also with self-sacrifice and hard work. What it all boils down to is simply this, you only get out of a marriage what you put into it. Tom L. Eisenman wrote:

> Marriage is like a good retirement plan. As long as you keep the deposits flowing, the account grows. The marriage develops like compound interest over time. Small investments of love and nurture reap great dividends in relational happiness.

Marriage is indeed an investment, like a good retirement plan. However, unlike a retirement plan, you don't have to wait until you're 65 to receive the benefits. Indeed, you must not wait!

To give you another analogy, your marriage is like a garden. If you neglect to look after it properly, weeds will start to grow. If you ignore the weeds, they will eventually take over the entire garden and will suffocate and choke to death all the beautiful flowers and fruits that once grew there. Often, when this happens, some men look over the garden fence and figure that the grass might be greener in his neighbour's garden, but it never is! (Sooner or later, weeds grow there as well.) As the author J. John writes, "The grass is not greener over that side of the fence. The grass is not greener over this side of the fence. The grass is greener where you water it!" The same is true when it comes to marriage. The marriage relationship is greener and produces more fruit when you water it.

So now, if I may, let me offer you a few simple pointers or suggestions for weeding and making the grass greener in your own marriage garden:

Marriage Garden Counselling

♦ Communication is, without doubt, the most important ingredient in a healthy marriage. Talk to your wife and just as importantly, if not more so, listen to her.

♦ Show affection. Hug her daily (in a non-sexual manner).

♦ Go for a walk together and hold hands.

♦ Switch off the TV and reminisce about the good old times. Get out your old photo albums and your home-shot camcorder video collection.

♦ Form the habit of spending one night a week together, every week, maybe enjoy a meal or go to the movies together.

♦ Write love notes or messages. Often a few words can speak volumes.

♦ Say these three little words often, "I love you."

♦ Develop a hobby, interest or past-time that you can do together. Learn a new language. Take a study course together.

♦ Exercise together. Go swimming, cycling, jogging or maybe go to the gym together.

♦ Give her a good back rub or a foot massage.

♦ Do the dishes or, at least, help out and do them together.

♦ True love never runs straight and sometimes a disagreement will end up in a quarrel or an argument. The Bible tells us, "Do not let the sun go down while you are still angry." By that, I take it to mean that it's okay to fall out now and again, just as long as you don't forget the best part... to kiss and make up afterwards! Sometimes it's difficult to make the first move and apologise but remember, a leader is meant to lead. Remember also that no one ever choked swallowing their pride!

Well, that's about all for now. I hope that you have enjoyed reading these letters as much as I've enjoyed writing them. As you are aware, it has become customary for me to try and incorporate an appropriate verse or poem in my letters and so to finish off, I'll leave you with this one on the subject of marriage (author anonymous):

The Art of Marriage

A good marriage must be created.
In a marriage, it's the little things that are the big things.
It is never being too old to hold hands.
It is remembering to say "I love you", at least once each day.
It is never going to sleep angry.
It is having a mutual sense of values and common objectives.
It is standing together and facing the world.
It is forming a circle of love that gathers in the whole family.
It is speaking words of appreciation and demonstrating gratitude in thoughtful ways.

It is having the capacity to forgive and forget.
It is giving each other an atmosphere in which each can grow.
It is a common search for the good and the beautiful.
It is not only marrying the right person,
It is also being the right partner.

I trust that you will be the right partner and that you will use the techniques and lessons contained in these letters to maximise your potential and live a long, happy, healthy and prosperous life. May God bless you in your efforts. Until next time then...

I remain yours cordially,

Uncle Bob

May the road rise to meet you.
May the wind be always at your back.
May the sun shine warm upon your face,
the rains fall soft upon your fields and,
until we meet again,
may God hold you in the palm of his hand.

(An Irish blessing)

INDEX

IAN SEYMOUR is available for speaking engagements, sales training seminars and consultancy appointments, internationally. He is also always happy to hear from his readers. If you would like to contact him, write to:

R. Ian Seymour
P.O. Box 3019 Wokingham
Berkshire RG40 4GA
England
Fax: 44 118 973 1857
Email: Ian.Seymour@btinternet.com